THE SHOP AT SLY CORNER

THE SHOP AT SLY CORNER

Edward Percy

WARNER CHAPPELL PLAYS

LONDON

A Time Warner Company

THE SHOP AT SLY CORNER
First published in 1946
by Warner Chappell Plays Ltd (pka English Theatre Guild Ltd.)
129 Park Street, London W1Y 3FA

This edition reprinted 1993
Copyright © 1946 by Edward Percy

ISBN 0 85676 087 0

Printed by Commercial Colour Press, London E7

THE SHOP AT SLY CORNER was first presented at the St Martin's Theatre, London, on 11th April, 1945, with the following cast:

DESCIUS HEISS	Keneth Kent
ARCHIE FELLOWES	John Carol
MARGARET HEISS	Victoria Hopper
JOAN DEAL	Joyce Heron
MATHILDE HEISS	Cathleen Nesbitt
MRS CATT	Ada Reeve
Robert Graham	William Roderick
CORDER MORRIS	Ernest Jay
STEVE HUBBARD	Rowland Bartrop
JOHN ELLIOT	Deryck Guyler

Directed by Henry Kendall

The action of the play takes place in a room at the back of a London shop.

ACT ONE: A Friday evening in August.

ACT TWO: A Sunday evening in the following winter.

ACT THREE: The following Tuesday morning.

ACT I

*A room at the back of a shop, in a pleasantly unfrequented
by-way of South London - the shop is that of a jeweller,
silversmith and antique dealer, but it is chiefly a curiosity
shop. It belongs to an old Alsatian emigré, long domiciled in
England,* DESCIUS HEISS, *and has for many years been
something of a landmark in its neighbourhood.*

*The room is large and is used partly as a store, partly as an
office, partly as a jeweller's workshop and partly even as a
sitting room. The wallpaper is reddish in tone and was
varnished years ago. Very little of it is visible however, for
much of the wall space is taken up by old pictures and
miniatures, an old oak dresser stacked with china, bronzes,
Sheffield plate and the like; pieces of armour and a motley
collection of weapons and Eastern implements, and one or
two oddments of faded tapestry. There is an atmosphere of
dust and untidiness. To the left stretches a wall in which
there is a door giving into the shop. The upper half of this
door is of glass and a green curtain can be pulled over the
panes. Further to the rear, up a short flight of balustraded
steps, is another doorway through which a passage leads to
the living rooms of the building. In the centre of the back
wall is the fireplace. It is surrounded by a commonplace
mantelpiece, flanked by two pilasters, and the chimney
aperture has been covered in by a sheet of black painted iron
to prevent the warmth of a fixed electric stove escaping up
the chimney. To the left of the mantelpiece is a large
jeweller's safe let into the wall. To the right, across the
corner in a fairly deep recess, is a workshop sink with a
built-in cupboard beneath it. Above the sink is a window
looking out on to a sly suburban street. A greasy yellow blind
and heavy red plush curtains can be drawn over this window,
if desired.*

*Along the wall to the left are some suits of armour on stands.
There is a Louis XVI settee in guilt and worn rose brocade;
there are one or two specimen tapestries and Ormolu chairs,
and some fine period English oak. The effect is that of a
dingy but attractive and rather amusing museum. It is an
evening in late August. The sun streams in through the*

window. Yet, oddly enough, the electric stove is turned full on.

Downstage, to the left, stands a large, carved, flat-topped knee-hole desk with a swivel chair behind it. The desk is used partly as a workshop table. On the "room" side of it is a fine armchair. The owner of the emporium is seated at the desk. On the desk to his left, stands a radio which is switched on. An orchestral concert of classical music is playing. It is a fine set, and the music sounds well.

DESCIUS HEISS *is a powerfully-built man of about sixty, a little inclining to "embonpoint." He has a remarkable face, rugged and lined with a hint of the Semitic in character, and fine lustrous dark eyes. He has a leonine head of grey hair, brushed back from his face. There is the suggestion of a slightly debased Beethoven about him. He wears a worn brown velveteen jacket, a white shirt with a soft collar and a black bow and old fashioned pepper-and-salt trousers which fit closely but comfortably around his muscular legs. He is quick in his movements and speech, and very much on the alert mentally. He has an easy, kindly bonhomie; he is fond of cracking his little jokes and is a bit of a "character". But you feel there is much more behind him than that - a certain greatness and depth of feeling, and perhaps, a certain ruthlessness. A jeweller's scale and weights, a tray of oddments of jewellery, a reading lamp and a telephone are in front of him. He has a jeweller's eyeglass in his eye and is examining the stones in a ring. When he speaks there is a trace of a foreign accent in his pronunciation and turn of phrase - only a trace though. A nearby church clock with chimes strikes the hour.*

ARCHIE FELLOWES *enters from the shop. He is the jeweller's assistant, and is worth a careful look. He is a good-looking boy of twenty or twenty-one erring on the side of effeminacy. He has a pale face and thin red lips. His eyes have a way of looking out of their corners. He is dressed neatly but shabbily in a suit he has outgrown. His manner is superior, but there is an attitude of indefinable insolence about him. He has an old fashioned brooch in his hand. He comes and stands before the desk. At first,* DESCIUS, *engrossed in the music, does not see him. Then he looks up.*

ARCHIE   An old girl's just -

DESCIUS   Oh - you? Wait! (*Turns down the radio to a soft note.*) Well? What is it?

ARCHIE   An old girl's just brought this in, guv'nor. Asks a couple of quid for it.

DESCIUS   (*taking the brooch and examining it perfunctorily*) Trumpery. A couple of quid? (*He puts it down.*) I don't want it. (*He takes it up once again.*) Well - twenty three and six, if she likes.

ARCHIE   (*muttering under his breath*) You'll give yourself away one of these days.

            (*He takes up the brooch.*)

DESCIUS   What did you say? (*Louder.*) What did you say?

ARCHIE   I said you'd give yourself away one of these days.

DESCIUS   How dare you! If I have any more of your insolence you go. See? Now, get out!

            (ARCHIE *goes.* DESCIUS *turns up the radio and continues his work. After a moment* ARCHIE *returns with the brooch.*)

            Wait! (*He switches off the radio.*) Well?

ARCHIE   She says if it's the best you can do.

            (ARCHIE *lays down the brooch. The old man takes it up.*)

DESCIUS   Pah! Victorian pinchbeck.

            (*He tosses it on to the tray before him. This time* ARCHIE *takes it up.*)

ARCHIE   Oh, I don't know. I'd call it rather beautiful.

                     (*He lays it down again, gracefully, insolently.*
                     DESCIUS *looks up in surprise. His eyes flash.*)

DESCIUS   (*satirically*) So that is your opinion? I thank
                     you.

                     (*Quite unmoved,* ARCHIE *saunters back into
                     the shop.* DESCIUS *glances after him angrily.
                     Then he picks up the brooch once more and
                     looks closely at it with his glass in his eye. As
                     he does so, two young women enter from the
                     house door. The first is a lovely girl,*
                     MARGARET, *the old man's daughter. She is
                     about twenty three. There is nothing of the
                     foreigner about her except that she is dark
                     and has an interesting, rather withdrawn
                     personality. She is a woman who lives very
                     much on her emotions, but they are deep and
                     true. She is artistic and sensitive, a musician
                     by profession, her instrument the violin. The
                     other girl is her great friend* JOAN DEAL. *She
                     is a taking blonde with a touch of the Cockney
                     in her composition. She has a strong vein of
                     pert humour, but is very commonsensical. She
                     is a chemist and works in a laboratory. They
                     are both dressed for an outing, but not
                     expensively. They enter with a good deal of
                     gusto, and their appearance seems to fill the
                     crowded and rather sinister room with an
                     effervescent light.*)

MARGARET   Hullo, Daddy! (*She sees the brooch in his
                     hand.*) What a pretty thing!

DESCIUS   (*handing it to her with a smile*) You like it?

MARGARET   (*examining it*) It's charming.

DESCIUS   You have it.

                     (*He rises and fastens it on her dress. She
                     kisses him affectionately.*)

MARGARET	You darling!
JOAN	I wish my father was a jeweller.
DESCIUS	You wouldn't if you knew.
JOAN	Why not?
DESCIUS	It's a dog's life. And I'm not a jeweller really. If I were, I should be so thin you could not see me sideways.
MARGARET	(*laughing*) Darling, what nonsense you talk!
DESCIUS	It's not nonsense, my sweet. If I make myself a herring for my breakfast I am satisfied. That is all I get out of my jewellery trade. If I want a porterhouse steak, I must sell an antique - which reminds me - is your aunt ready?
MARGARET	She's just coming.
DESCIUS	Then I'd better give you the tickets. (*He goes to the safe and begins to unlock it.*)
JOAN	I'm afraid I've never said thank you for the treat your giving me, Mr Heiss.
DESCIUS	(*not in the least rudely*) Oh, don't put yourself out. You're Margaret's friend. You're just a part of the story.
JOAN	Well, that's one way of looking at it!
DESCIUS	(*still with his back to them*) And it's the way I look at it.
MARGARET	Daddy! Do you realise you're being horribly rude?
DESCIUS	(*coming forward*) I, darling! Rude? No!
JOAN	The fact is, I'm in and out of this house so often that he forgets to take any notice of me.

DESCIUS	Ah! Like Mr Chesterton's postman. Invisible because everyone is so accustomed to him! We are always glad to see you here, Joan. We are always glad *not* to notice you, because you and Margaret have been friends since you were so high, and we want you to go on being friends.
JOAN	I expect my dad would say the same about Margaret.
DESCIUS	How nice we all are to each other this evening!
	(*He laughs and returns to the safe for the tickets.*)
MARGARET	I say, it's hot in here! I can't think how you can stand it.
DESCIUS	Well, if you don't like it, open the window.
	(MARGARET *throws the window up.*)
JOAN	Do you really want this stove full on?
MARGARET	(*noticing it, too*) The stove? Oh, *Daddy*!
DESCIUS	Is the stove on? (*He turns - he has the tickets in his hand.*) So it is. Now, how comes that?
JOAN	You don't really need it, do you?
DESCIUS	If you don't like it, switch it off.
MARGARET	(*she is by the fireplace*) Daddy, the wall's quite hot! You ought to have the electric people here. There may be a short circuit.
DESCIUS	(*joining her and himself feeling the wall*) The wall - hot? Tch! Tch! Yes, I must have that seen to. Turn it off at once. There's a good girl. (*She does so.*) Now, here are the tickets.

Let's be sure there's no mistake. Are they for the second house? Yes! That's all right.

MARGARET   (*taking them*) Oh, a box! How thrilling!

DESCIUS   (*returning to the safe and relocking it*) Well, it is such a very good play.

JOAN   (*looking at the tickets with* MARGARET) "Ladies In Retirement."

DESCIUS   It's all about a murder.

JOAN   I'm so glad! I adore crime on the stage. It always makes me feel so moral.

DESCIUS   A murder committed by a woman. A very clever woman. But she made one mistake.

MARGARET   What was that?

DESCIUS   You will see. You will see.

(*An old lady with a definite Jewish trait bustles in from the house door. This is* MATHILDE HEISS, DESCIUS' *sister. She is stout and shrewd with quick, black eyes. She, too, is dressed for the theatre, but very much more elaborately than the girls. She is wearing a démondé and violently coloured evening gown of silk. She has a white lace shawl round her head and a rather moth-eaten black fur coat over her dress. She wears a good deal of old fashioned jewellery. She is busy buttoning on a pair of white kid gloves which might with advantage be whiter.*)

DESCIUS   Ah! Here is Aunt Mathilde! All dressed up and somewhere to go!

MATHILDE   I'm not late. Am I?

MARGARET   The taxi isn't here yet.

MATHILDE   I've left a pickled mackerel for your supper,
            Descius. Mrs Catt knows all about it.

DESCIUS   (*in facetious dismay*) That sounds bad.

MATHILDE   It's quite all right. She never touches
            anything with vinegar on it. Chickens - yes.
            Or with sheeps and beefs she would not be
            safe - no. But she will not steal anything in
            vinegar. Because it turns her stomach.

MARGARET   (*laughing*) Poor Mrs Catt!

DESCIUS   Oh, she is a great sufferer.

MATHILDE   (*volubly*) If it is not her stomach it is her
            bowels; if it is not her bowels it is her feet; if
            it is not her feet it is her asthma. I tell her she
            is a home from home for Incurables! (*To
            DESCIUS.*) Now you will like the mackerel
            because I have prepared it myself. With a bay
            leaf and plenty of peppercorns.

DESCIUS   And garlic, eh? Garlic! Oh you wonderful
            woman! (*Whimsically rueful.*) But then I
            cannot go kissing tonight.

MATHILDE   Kissing tonight! At your age! Phuh!

DESCIUS   I am going to spend a lovely evening, Joan.
            They're doing the Brandenburg Concerto on
            the wireless. Don't you envy me?

JOAN   Lord, no. I'd much rather be going to your
            murder play.

DESCIUS   But then you're not fond of music. To me
            music means all that your Bunsen burners and
            your microscopes mean to you.

JOAN   That's different. That's my job.

DESCIUS   Exactly! And if there had been more money in
            it, music would have been *my* job. (*Simply.*)

Do you know what is the loveliest thing in my life? (*Putting his arms around* MARGARET.) That Margaret here should be a musician.

MARGARET   Darling, that's a sweet thing to say.

DESCIUS   When I sit in the stalls and look up at her playing her violin at a concert, I think sometimes she must be a sorceress. (*Momentarily darkening.*) She coaxes my soul out of my so vile self. (*Changing.*) But we are all like that, all. (*With a sudden smile.*) Except Margaret. (*Sharply, with a complete change of tone.*) What do you want?

(*For* ARCHIE *has entered from the shop.*)

ARCHIE   I've just sold that little Adams' tea caddy, guv'nor. For four pounds.

DESCIUS   For four pounds? Aha! We shall make a salesman of you yet.

ARCHIE   I saw the customer meant to have it so I put up the price.

DESCIUS   (*pulling* ARCHIE'S *ear playfully*) I shall have to reconsider my decision not to give you that extra rise of five shillings a week you asked for.

ARCHIE   (*obviously pleased*) Thank you very much, sir. I shan't say no.

DESCIUS   Don't jump to conclusions. I *have* reconsidered it. We stay where we are.

(*An ugly look flashes across* ARCHIE'S *face.*)

ARCHIE   (*icily*) That's just too bad.

MARGARET   (*pleasantly*) Good evening, Archie.

ARCHIE   (*eyeing her admiringly*) Good evening, Miss Margaret. (*To* JOAN.) Good evening, Miss.

JOAN   Good evening.

ARCHIE   You're all looking very smart, if I may say so.

JOAN   (*rising and moving to the table behind sofa
                for a cigarette*) We're going to enjoy
                ourselves.

ARCHIE   And why not, if you've got the chance? You
                look like a bit of gay Paree, Miss.

JOAN   If you really want to know the truth, I'm the
                front cover of last month's "Vogue".

ARCHIE   (*admiringly*) Nice stuff!

MARGARET   And what do I look like, Archie?

ARCHIE   You look like yourself, Miss. What could be
                nicer?

JOAN   (*sitting on the sofa*) We're off to the theatre.

MATHILDE   And we're going to see "Ladies in
                Retirement".

ARCHIE   (*with a curl of his lip*) Oh, that rotten old
                thing!

DESCIUS   (*annoyed*) "That rotten old thing!" What do
                you mean? It's a very good play.

ARCHIE   I suppose one might call it good theatre.

DESCIUS   (*flaring*) What are you? A shop boy or a
                dramatic critic?

ARCHIE   If you really want to know the technical term,
                Mr Heiss, I believe it's called "shop
                assistant".

                (*He sidles insolently back into the shop. He
                shuts the door behind him. There is an angry
                pause, then* DESCIUS *explodes.*)

DESCIUS   He's a sissy! That's what he is, I believe - a sissy! (*Mimicking* ARCHIE.) "I suppose one might call it good theatre." What does he know about the theatre?

MARGARET   Don't be so unreasonable. Why shouldn't he know something about the theatre?

DESCIUS   Because I know, on what I pay him, that he can't afford to go to the theatre!

MATHILDE   Why must you always drop down on Archie, Descius? He is a good boy. He is one of the best boys we have ever had. He is well-behaved. He is respectful. He is quiet.

DESCIUS   He is quiet, yes. But he is sly. If he were not so cheap, I should have kicked him out weeks ago.

MATHILDE   (*volubly*) Why do you call him sly? The boy only wants to get on. He tries. It may be that for a boy he is too much of a girl. But that's nothing new.

DESCIUS   He is not only sly, Mathilde, he is hard. He is selfish. He is cruel, too.

MARGARET   (*almost indignantly*) How *can* you say that?

DESCIUS   Oh, I know. I have ways of knowing people.

MARGARET   (*bantering*) You and your ways!

(*And so the little continental quarrel works itself up.*)

MATHILDE   It is only your father's fool of a temper, my love. (*In an excitable crescendo.*) What does it matter if Archie is hard or selfish or cruel or sly? What he does in his spare time is no business of ours. Where else should we get anyone like him for twenty five shillings a

week and nothing found? It is always the
same here! We can never keep our assistants.
(*To* DESCIUS.) You are forever upsetting them
- you old crab louse!

DESCIUS   Crab louse!

MATHILDE   Crab louse! But I warn you - if you get rid of
Archie I will have nothing to do with it! I will
not help in the shop! I'll wash my hands of it!
I am on strike!

DESCIUS   (*roaring*) Are you the mistress of this house?
Or am I?

(*Into the squabble has drifted the forlorn
figure of* MRS CATT. *She is about sixty years
of age. She wears felt bedroom slippers and
walks with a hobble. Every work, every
movement, suggests that she is - or would like
to be - a hospital case.*)

MRS CATT   If you please, sir, 'ere's Dr Graham!

MARGARET   (*with delight*) Robert! Where?

MRS CATT   Payin' 'is taxi - with my last half-crown.

MATHILDE   Robert? Home?

(ROBERT GRAHAM *enters like a hurricane from
the house door. He is a breezy, attractive
young nautical doctor. He is wearing his
uniform. He is a surgeon aboard a liner
engaged on the Eastern trade route. He comes
running down the few steps, swinging a
suitcase. He is* MARGARET'S *fiancé and is also
a great favourite with the rest of the family.*)

ROBERT   Hello, everyone!

MARGARET   Rob!

ROBERT   Hullo, my sweet! (*They embrace.*) Hullo,
Poppa. Hullo Aunt Mathilde. Hullo Joan. (*To*
MRS CATT.) I did say hullo to you, didn't I?

MRS CATT	(*going into a thin cackle of laughter as she departs*) Gracious, yes! When I opened the door to 'im I thought 'e was goin' to kiss me instanter!
DESCIUS	Well, Robert! This is a surprise! What's brought you back?
ROBERT	My ship. We're ahead of schedule.
DESCIUS	Well, you're just in time to go to the theatre with them all!
MARGARET	We've got a box!
ROBERT	Too good to be true.
MATHILDE	(*sentimentally*) Aren't you going to kiss *me*, Robert?
ROBERT	You, my charmer? (*He kisses her.*) Listen, darling. You and I are going to get into a huddle one of these days and make Margaret jealous.
MATHILDE	(*adoringly*) Oh, how I wish you meant it!
MARGARET	(*to* ROBERT) But what have you been doing? Tell us!
ROBERT	Nothing to tell. Voyage too deadly dull for words. I hadn't a patient. I've forgotten all my medicine. I shall make Mrs Catt sail with me next time so I can have someone to treat.
MARGARET	(*fondling him*) Rob darling, don't ever let me know when you're coming home again, will you? Then I can always live on the edge of a thrilling surprise!
ROBERT	I hope you'll feel like that when we're married. Because some sailors' wives, you know, *do* get taken by surprise.

MARGARET   (*catching his mood*) Oh, I shall post a
               lookout!

ROBERT   Good for you!

MATHILDE   And you've come all the way from Singapore
               without letting us know?

ROBERT   Damn it, I wrote from Suez!

MARGARET   We haven't had it.

ROBERT   Then I'm here before my news.

DESCIUS   (*playfully*) Robert, tell me. Have you been
               faithful to my little girl all the time you've
               been away?

ROBERT   (*heartily*) Sure!

DESCIUS   I have my doubts. Your eyes are too bright.

ROBERT   Well, I've got something to show you.

               (ROBERT *has set his suitcase upon the desk and
               begins to open it.*)

DESCIUS   What have you got there?

ROBERT   Some things I picked up in Singapore. From
               an old Chinaman.

DESCIUS   Ah, let's have a look.

ROBERT   You've got to sell 'em for me and make me a
               profit, Poppa!

MARGARET   And then it's to be paid over to me!

ROBERT   Take the words out of my mouth, won't you?

               (*He takes some objects from his suitcase
               wrapped in Oriental newspapers. He unwraps
               them.*)

MARGARET   (*in wonderment*) Bronze frogs!

ROBERT   (*explaining them*) Incense burners. You know,
                   for joss sticks. (*To* DESCIUS.) Not quite a pair.
                   But they'd pass as one.

DESCIUS   (*admiring them*) Yes. Very nice. (*To* AUNT
                   MATHILDE.) Look, Mathilde - big fellows. Like
                   our frogs in Alsace.

ROBERT   (*producing a miniature teapot in black
                   bronze*) Mandarin's bronze teapot - signed by
                   the artist.

DESCIUS   Ah, this is a good one, Robert. This is very
                   nice.

ROBERT   Look, my charmer! See what I've brought for
                   you!

MATHILDE   What is it, Robert?

ROBERT   A Geisha girl's night-dress. (*He takes a
                   necklace from the bag and holds it up.*)

MATHILDE   Oh, you naughty boy! Thank you, Robert.

                   (*She takes the necklace, shows it to* JOAN *and
                   then moves across to a mirror and puts it on.*)

ROBERT   (*taking a large Buddha from his bag*) What do
                   you think? Showy? From Burma.

DESCIUS   (*receiving it*) No, Robert - from Birmingham.
                   Oh well - perhaps I can palm him off on some
                   intellectual Christian - except that intellectual
                   Christians are so scarce.

ROBERT   Well, here's a curiosity, if you like! Savage's
                   blowpipe from Senegambia.

DESCIUS   (*handling it with interest*) It looks like one of
                   my favourite cigars.

ROBERT   (*holding up a little native box*) And a couple
              of poison darts.

DESCIUS   (*opening the box*) My! Aren't they like a
              tomcat's claws?

ROBERT   (*sharply*) Don't touch 'em!

DESCIUS   Why?

ROBERT   They're acacia thorns. That shiny stuff on the
              points is curare.

JOAN   (*examining them with interest*) Curare!

DESCIUS   Enter the scientist.

MARGARET   What *is* curare?

ROBERT   It's a strychnine compound mixed with
              several poisonous gums. It's deadly, and
              keeps its strength for years.

JOAN   Is it true that curare's really instantaneous?

ROBERT   Practically.

JOAN   None of the poison manuals seems to know
              much about it. I'd like to analyse one of these
              - may I?

ROBERT   Sure. But you'll have to buy the whole outfit.
              We can't can't split the parcel, can we,
              Poppa? What's the lowest - blowpipe *and*
              darts?

DESCIUS   Three pounds. (*To* JOAN, *jocularly.*) Two
              pounds ten - and it's yours.

JOAN   (*with a twinkle*) You're unlucky, Mr Heiss.
              It's still yours.

ROBERT   You'll have to warn anyone buying it, Poppa.

DESCIUS   Splendid! That will send the price up. It will
              be quite safe with me, Robert. I shall reserve
              it for a collector.

MRS CATT   (*entering*) Did you know as the taxi wot you
                ordered 'as been standin' outside the last ten
                minutes tickin' up your thruppences?

MARGARET   (*suddenly remembering the theatre*) We shall
                be late for the show!

DESCIUS   (*to* MRS CATT) Why didn't you tell us?

MRS CATT   (*sadly, as she fades away into the passage*) I
                thought you knew.

DESCIUS   Never think, you fool! Only fools think!

MRS CATT   How right you are. (*She disappears.*)

                (*Immediately everything becomes bustle and
                hurry.*)

MARGARET   Come along, Aunt Mathilde!

ROBERT   Sure you've room for me?

MARGARET   We're not going without you!

DESCIUS   (*to* ROBERT) We will talk all these over when
                you come back, Robert.

JOAN   (*as she goes*) Enjoy your Brandenburg
                Concerto, Mr Heiss!

MATHILDE   (*lingering to lean over the little balustrade*)
                And if you do not like that pickled mackerel,
                I shall never make you another!

DESCIUS   (*shouting*) Is that a threat or a promise? Have
                a good time. Enjoy yourselves. You haven't
                forgotten the key?

                (*They have all gone. The telephone rings.*
                DESCIUS *lifts the receiver. As he does so,*
                ARCHIE, *carrying the sales book and the till
                drawer, enters from the shop. He stands in the
                doorway listening.* DESCIUS *does not perceive
                him.*)

DESCIUS   (*speaking into the telephone*) Yes. Yes,
                        speaking. Oh, yes. I recognise your voice.
                        Where are you speaking from? Round the
                        corner? Good. I'm quite ready for you.

                        (ARCHIE *stealthily withdraws.* DESCIUS *puts
                        down the receiver. A church clock in the
                        neighbourhood chimes the half hour.* DESCIUS
                        *moves to the radio and switches it on. The
                        Brandenberg Concerto comes through. He
                        listens to the broadcast for a moment, beating
                        time with his hands. Then he starts to set
                        ROBERT'S curios in various positions on the
                        table and a cabinet behind his chair. First,
                        the two incense burners, then the Mandarin's
                        teapot which he examines admiringly and
                        places most carefully in the centre of the
                        table. Afterwards he takes up the Buddha
                        which he decides to set in the position
                        occupied by the bust of Beethoven on the
                        cabinet. He removes the bust to the table, sets
                        the Buddha on the cabinet, regards it
                        disapprovingly for a moment and then
                        replaces Beethoven and throws the Buddha to
                        the floor with an exclamation of impatience.
                        He then picks up the box of darts, opens it,
                        and examines them carefully through his
                        magnifying glass. He closes the box and sets
                        it down on the radio cabinet. At that moment
                        ARCHIE re-enters, still carrying the sales book
                        and the till drawer. He stands behind* DESCIUS.
                        DESCIUS, *unaware of his presence, picks up the
                        blow pipe, holds it up to the light, looks
                        through it and then puts it to his lips. He
                        suddenly realises that* ARCHIE *is behind him.
                        He sets the blow pipe down on the radio
                        cabinet beside the box of darts.*)

DESCIUS   Wait. (*He switches off the radio.*) Well?

ARCHIE   It's eight-thirty, Guv'nor. I'm just going. I've
                        shut the shutters. Here's the till and the sales
                        book.

DESCIUS   Aha? Yes, yes, yes, yes, yes.

ARCHIE   Whew! Some heat in here.

               (ARCHIE *puts down the book and till on a chair
               below the sofa.*)

DESCIUS   It is still August, Archie. The sun is only just
               setting. You might notice it if you looked.

ARCHIE   There's no harm in making a remark, is there?

DESCIUS   None whatever. (*Coming close to him in a
               rather ugly way.*) But I do not like some of
               your remarks, my little Archie. I shall have to
               take you down a peg or two one day.

ARCHIE   (*lightly*) Before you can do that you'll have to
               put me up a peg or two, won't you?

               (DESCIUS *suddenly grips* ARCHIE'S *arms
               strongly just above the elbows, pinning them
               to his sides, and looks up into his face with a
               strange demonic intensity.*)

DESCIUS   Listen, my little Archie - I call you "little"
               because you are a very little person - I am old
               enough to be your grandfather, but I am
               strong as a lion. Don't tempt me to use my
               strength on you, will you, my little friend?

ARCHIE   (*penetratingly*) Why do you want to make me
               afraid of you?

               (DESCIUS'S *manner changes, almost as if he
               realised he had gone too far. He releases the
               boy with a friendly smile.*)

DESCIUS   Make you afraid of me? I don't! But I want to
               make you disciplined. you are too
               undisciplined, boy. You are very
               undisciplined. And now, that is enough
               curtain lectures for one evening. (*Good*

	humouredly.) Run along, Archie - and enjoy yourself.
ARCHIE	Will you lock the shutter door after me?
DESCIUS	I will.
ARCHIE	Good night, then Guv'nor.
DESCIUS	Good night, Archie.

(ARCHIE *goes.* DESCIUS *stands looking after him for a moment. Then, with an instinctive shudder of dislike, he crosses himself and picks up the tray of trinkets from the desk which he places in the safe with the till and the sales book.*)

(*to himself, obviously preoccupied*) Let me see . . . Lock the shutter door . . . Ah, yes, I go and do that.

(*He switches off the radio. He goes into the shop, and we hear the iron shutter pulled down.* MRS CATT *enters from the house. She comes to the desk.*)

| MRS CATT | If you please, there's a . . . Oh! (*Seeing nobody is there. She stands for a moment scratching her head.*) Oh! (*She sees some papers on the floor near the couch. She picks them up, grumbling.*) Wot a 'arum-scarum joint! It might be the Old Kent Road on a Saturday night. |

(DESCIUS *returns. He shuts the door into the shop, then he sees* MRS CATT.)

| DESCIUS | What do you mean - slobbering about the place in those golosher slippers? |
| MRS CATT | (*sorrowfully*) I can't 'elp it, sir. It's me feet. They're somethink chronic. Look 'ow me ankles is swolled. Of course, that's me 'eart, that is. But it don't 'elp me feet. There's |

times I 'ave to sit down and daydream they terrify me so.

DESCIUS   (*coming to his desk*) Haven't you got a wireless? Why don't you tune in to some lovely music and forget all your ailments for five minutes?

MRS CATT   (*mournfully*) I only listens to the noos. But I'm best when I gets an attack of asthma. That do take me mind off me feet. (*She shuffles to the door, then stops suddenly.*) Oh, I did mean ter say there's a gentleman called - a Mr. Morris.

DESCIUS   (*exasperated*) Well, why couldn't you say so before?

MRS CATT   You put it out o' me 'ead talking about me feet.

DESCIUS   (*eagerly*) Well, off you go. Show the gentleman in! And look - when you've done that you can go. Do you understand? I'll get my own supper.

MRS CATT   Very good, sir.

DESCIUS   You go right off, see? Take the evening off. Take the night off. Take everything off. I can't stand you slippering about the place.

MRS CATT   No. Of course you can't. You can't be expected to. I finds it difficult to stand meself sometimes.

(DESCIUS *closes the window and draws the curtains as she mumbles herself away. Then he switches on the electric stove. He returns to his desk, switches on his reading lamp and then takes from a drawer a revolver and lays it on the desk, covering it with his white handkerchief.* MRS CATT *returns, showing in* CORDER MORRIS.)

MRS CATT   Mr Morris, sir.

                  (CORDER MORRIS *is a man of about thirty,*
                  sleek-haired and heavy-jowled, but with an
                  upright, lithe figure. He has large, black eyes
                  and fairly heavy eyebrows. He wears smart,
                  ready-made clothes and thin-soled patent
                  leather shoes. You can meet his type in any
                  second-rate West End cocktail bar. He might
                  be a middle-weight boxer or all-in wrestler;
                  he might be a greyhound trainer; he is a
                  crook.)

DESCIUS   (*welcomingly*) Ah, my dear Morris! How are
                  you?

MORRIS   Suppose I mustn't grumble.

DESCIUS   How goes the world?

MORRIS   I don't know - till we've talked.

                  (MRS CATT, *who has retired, puts her head*
                  round the door.)

MRS CATT   (*in a soft, weary voice*) *'Scuse me . . .*

DESCIUS   *What is it now?*

MRS CATT   You was serious when you said you didn't
                  want me, wasn't you?

DESCIUS   (*going quickly to the door*) Yes, I was!

                  (MRS CATT'S *head is rapidly withdrawn. She*
                  shuts the door. Then he rejoins MORRIS,
                  roaring with laughter.)

MORRIS   *Same old dear, I see.*

DESCIUS   (*nodding*) *I couldn't have anyone better.*

MORRIS   (*with a little shudder*) I need a bit more sex
                  appeal around me. She'd put me off my bed.

(*A street door is heard to shut loudly.*)

(*nervously*) What's that?

DESCIUS She has gone.

(*He goes to the window, parts the curtains, lifts a corner of the blind and peers out.*)

Yes. There she goes. In a beeline for "The Bricklayer's Arms." (*Turning to* MORRIS, *carefully.*) Now, my friend, shall we talk business, or shall we talk business?

MORRIS Have you given the doings the once-over?

DESCIUS (*taking a tiny black velvet bag from the safe*) Yes. Yes. I've got them here. I've removed the settings. Ah, did I leave the door open? I am nervous of draughts at my age.

(*He shuts the shop door, forgetting that he has shut it once before. Then he spreads a sheet of white paper on the desk and empties the contents of the bag upon it. A heap of glittering loose gems falls out.*)

I suppose this was the Porchester Place job?

MORRIS Yes.

DESCIUS There is a lot of it. But it is very old fashioned. (*He searches about among the stones with a jeweller's forceps.*) And most of the diamonds are Indians. Only here and there a South African.

MORRIS That's right. Blow on the goods.

DESCIUS (*looking up, quite sincerely*) I never do that, Morris. You will acknowledge that - when we know one another better. (*Returning to the gems.*) All rose stones, you see. Not a square cut among the lot.

> (*They are now seated one each side of the desk, with the jewels between them.*)

> What do you think they were worth?

MORRIS   To you?

DESCIUS   No, no! To buy in the open market? The gross value?

MORRIS   Sixteen hundred.

DESCIUS   (*slowly shaking his head*) No.

MORRIS   Look at that emerald. You couldn't buy that under a hundred and seventy quid.

DESCIUS   (*picking up the stone with the forceps and turning it over*) A hundred and ten. A hundred and twenty, perhaps. And that is the pick of the bunch.

MORRIS   What do you put the open market value?

DESCIUS   A thousand.

MORRIS   (*in disgust*) A thousand!

DESCIUS   Not a penny more.

MORRIS   You're trying to test me, you old . . . fox.

DESCIUS   (*slowly, eyeing him straightly*) I never do that. We've not had many deals together, Morris. But you know my terms. We arrive at the gross value. I give you twenty five per cent. In this case, two hundred and fifty pounds.

MORRIS   (*disgustedly*) Two hundred and fifty!

DESCIUS   There's not another fence in London who'll give you more than one sixth. That is why I succeed where others fail. I pay more. I'm safe. I work alone. And I never blackmail. If you don't like my price, you take away your goods. All is forgotten. If you don't come back to me - well, I shrug my shoulders.

"Open agreements openly arrived at" - that's my business principle.

MORRIS Two hundred and fifty quid! (*Holding up a bandaged finger.*) And I tore my bloody fingernail out on that gutter!

DESCIUS (*with a ghost of a smile*) It is a pity your trade does not come under the Industrial Insurance Act - but there it is.

(*There is a short, uneasy pause.*)

MORRIS Do you want this cursed stove on?

DESCIUS If you don't like it, shut it off.

(MORRIS *does so. He takes out a brilliant silk handkerchief and runs it round the inside of his collar.*)

MORRIS A sweltering night like this, too.

DESCIUS My daughter put it on. She's a chilly person. I don't notice the heat myself. I've lived in hot climates.

(*There is another pause.*)

MORRIS Can't you spring to three fifty?

(DESCIUS *does not reply. He makes a funnel out of the paper and runs the stones back into the velvet bag.*)

Three hundred?

DESCIUS (*holding out the bag*) There you are, Morris. Try Grizzard. Or Kritovsky.

MORRIS They're not worth another fifty to you?

DESCIUS Not another five pound note. Try somebody else. You're welcome. There'll be no ill feeling.

(MORRIS *takes the bag of jewels and turns
savagely on his heels. The old man's face is a
study in amused slyness.*)

Goodnight, Morris. Goodnight!

(MORRIS *goes to the door, then turns and
comes back. He tosses the bag onto the desk
in front of* DESCIUS.)

MORRIS   Ok, Two fifty then. Hand it over.

(DESCIUS *rises.*)

(*in a low voice, intensely*) D'you know what
it means to rob a house?

DESCIUS   No, dear boy. I'm not a thief. That's not my
function. (*He goes to the safe, and puts in the
jewels, then takes out a number of notes.*)

MORRIS   (*slowly, emphatically*) The watching. The
waiting. They're enough to get you down.
Then the getting in. You risk your life. A
false step may mean - number up. D'you
figure what that does to your nerves? You
may be shot if the bloke has a gun. If he
hasn't - if he's sly - if he keeps quiet - you
may have the cops on you. Two years' hard.
Three years' penal. You never know what
you're going to fall in for. Your guts are like
jelly. It's zero hour. You've got a gun -
loaded - very likely. A pull on the trigger -
just nerves, perhaps - and - where are you?
For the high jump, as like as not.

(DESCIUS *counts out the five notes, dealing
them out on the desk before him like cards. It
is the perfect anti-climax to* MORRIS'S
eloquence.)

DESCIUS   Fifty. Fifty. Fifty. Fifty. Fifty.

(MORRIS *takes them, produces his pocket book
and stuffs them in.*)

MORRIS   (*still aggrieved*) And you sit there and offer
                me twenty five percent!

DESCIUS   I shan't get more than fifty.

MORRIS   Granted. But who's doing the most? Who's
                bringing in the dough? You or me?

DESCIUS   Listen, Morris. I will tell you a little story.
                Nearly fifty years ago, in the town of Saint
                Dié in the Vosges, there lived a small boy. He
                was fourteen years old. His father was dead.
                He lived with his mother and some younger
                brothers and sisters. It was a hard winter.
                Work was scarce. It was a hungry winter, too.
                Even the wolves came down from the
                mountains into the outskirts of the town. One
                day, in a moment of temptation, this small
                boy stole a loaf out of a baker's basket. But
                he hadn't learnt to steal properly. He was
                caught. He was sentenced to fourteen months'
                imprisonment - one month, I suppose, for
                every year of his age. When he came out, his
                mother was dead. His little brothers and
                sisters - well, I don't know where they were.
                He drifted down to the south of France - to
                Marseilles. There he picked up quite easily
                with a young Apache gang. If you have done
                fourteen months in a French prison, you have
                a passport to Hell - visaed forever. One night
                there was a scuffle on the quay. A drunken
                sea captain was stabbed. He died. This boy -
                and two others - were arrested. Whether the
                boy had helped to kill the sea captain I don't
                know. It was too much of a melee. All the
                boys had knives. They were all found guilty.
                Two were guillotined. Our boy was sentenced
                for life. He was sent to Guiana - to Devil's
                Island. He escaped. He suffered terribly. At
                last he got to England. And started business in
                a small way. He began to get on. After a time
                he married a beautiful woman. She died when
                their child was born. He could never show her
                his back. He had to devise all sorts of excuses

so that he did not show her his back. Never - never.

MORRIS   (*intently - he has been following the story with keen interest*) Why?

DESCIUS   Oh, I beg your pardon - he had been flogged many times. Look!

           (*Suddenly he throws off his coat, loosens his collar and turns his back to* MORRIS. *The latter, fascinated, slowly pulls down the shirt from the shoulders. A look of horror grows across his face.*)

MORRIS   (*softly*) Gee!

           (DESCIUS *fastens up his shirt. He does not put on his coat.*)

DESCIUS   I tell you this, my dear Morris, so you may know that I, too, have paid the - er - subscription which crime demands from her followers.

MORRIS   (*quietly, admiringly*) You certainly have.

DESCIUS   Since then I have lived peaceably and honestly in good old England! God save the King! (*He sits once more at his desk.*)

MORRIS   (*with the flicker of a smile*) Did you say honestly?

DESCIUS   Well, honesty is a relative term. At all events, I've brought my daughter up to lead an honest life even if *I* can't. (*Sincerely.*) So I *do* know what thieves feel, Morris. I even know what it means to be adjudged guilty of murder. I have been through it all.

MORRIS   Aren't you taking a hell of a risk - telling me?

DESCIUS   No, Morris. I know men. I have learnt to know them. I have confidence in you. And now you will have confidence in me. I hope

we shall have many little transactions
together in future. (*He proffers him a box of
Havana cigars.*) Cigar?

MORRIS   Thanks. (*He takes one.*) No, Mr Heiss. You'll
              never hear of Corder Morris ratting on a pal.

DESCIUS   So I have been told. No. Don't bite it. The
              one thing you mustn't do to a good cigar is to
              bite it. I'm always telling my American
              friends that. You should pierce it with the
              unbusiness end of a match. So! (*He pierces
              the cigar with a match stick.*) It makes just
              the right size hole. Does not fray the leaf. (*He
              hands* MORRIS *the cigar, which he puts in his
              mouth.*) Let me give you a light. And now it
              would be well if you did not stay any longer.
              I don't suppose you've been watched, but one
              never knows.

MORRIS   Right. I'll be blowing. (*With a change of
              mood.*) To tell you the honest truth, I'm never
              sorry to get out of here.

DESCIUS   (*surprised*) Why?

MORRIS   I don't know. All this old stuff. Gives me the
              willies. It's like living in the Chamber of
              Horrors. (*He goes to the suits of armour.*)
              These coves, for instance. They look like
              ghosts. I hope to God they're hollow.

              (*He raps one breast plate with his knuckles.*)

DESCIUS   What do you mean?

MORRIS   I mean - I hope there isn't a nark inside any
              of 'em.

DESCIUS   None of the gentleman who wore these would
              have passed our modern police standards. The
              tallest is only five foot seven. That's a suit of
              Dutch armour. Let me sell it to you. Only
              seventy five pounds. (*Slyly.*) You have the
              money on you.

MORRIS   (*dryly*) Reckon he'd feel a bit homesick in a
                basement flat in Battersea.

DESCIUS   (*lightly*) Oh, it will come in for your country
                house when you have one.

MORRIS   What a hope!

DESCIUS   (*smiling*) Oh, just go on as you're going.
                You'll do. And I shall hope to see you again
                before long. But remember - gold and jewels.
                Nothing but gold and jewels. I never touch
                silver. Too much trouble and nothing in it.

MORRIS   (*slyly*) We all know *your* habits. (*Going past
                into the passage.*) Well, so long, Mr Heiss.
                I'll be seeing you.

DESCIUS   (*off*) Goodnight. Goodnight.

                (*The street door shuts.* DESCIUS *returns,
                humming. He turns his shirt sleeves up.*)

                Sur le pont d'Avignon
                L'on y danse, l'on y danse!
                Sur le pont d'Avignon
                L'on y danse tout en ronde!

                (*He goes to the cupboard under the sink and
                takes out a deep iron tray. He places this in
                the sink and turns on the tap above it, letting
                it fill with cold water. Then he approaches the
                fireplace and turns round a small miniature
                hanging on the wall beside it. This operates a
                hidden bolt, for the mantelpiece opens into
                the room like a door between its two pilasters.
                The clock and ornaments upon it are screwed
                in and so keep their balance. They look
                grotesque standing on the top of the open
                door. In the cavity of the chimney behind,
                which is fairly deep, is a moderate-sized
                electric furnace. It is burning and, now the
                door is opened, you can hear the faint hum of
                power. It is this which has made the room so*

hot. Beside the furnace stand a pair of crucible tongs, two pairs of small tongs, some crucibles and greased moulds, and, hanging on the wall, a black eye shade. DESCIUS *places one of the moulds on the hearth stone. Then he puts on the eye shade, and, taking up the crucible tongs, opens the furnace door and peers in. His figure is sharply illuminated by the fierce red glow as he crouches before it. He inserts the tongs and carefully draws out a small black crucible which is almost red-hot. He deftly pours its yellow contents into the waiting mould. Then he places the crucible in the recess together with the crucible tongs and his eye shade, and, pulling up the levers, shuts off the power. He then takes up the two pairs of smaller tongs - one in each hand - and prepares to lift the mould. As he is thus engaged,* ARCHIE *emerges from behind one of the suits of armour. He has hidden there under cover of darkness and has been spying on* DESCIUS. *He creeps up to the desk, stands behind it, and, removing the old man's handkerchief, picks up the revolver. Meanwhile* DESCIUS *has lifted up the mould with the tongs and lowers it into the tray of cold water. An almighty hissing arises from it. Noiselessly* ARCHIE *turns on the radio. As the hissing subsides, an orchestral selection of noisy jazz is playing very loudly, and then switched down to a soft accompaniment of the scene.* DESCIUS *swings around, to be confronted by* ARCHIE, *with the pistol in his hand.)*

DESCIUS   (*his voice so low, he can hardly be heard*) What do you want?

                (ARCHIE *does not answer.*)

                (*loudly, insistently*) What do you want?

ARCHIE   (*quietly*) I haven't quite made up my mind.

                (*Blackout.*)

ACT TWO

In the darkness, the notes of a violin are heard, playing the concluding passage of "Meditation" from Massenet's opera "Thais".

When the lights rise, the room is bright and cosy, and shut up for a winter evening. The electric stove is burning. JOAN *is standing by a little folding table laid for tea, buttering some crumpets she has just toasted.* ROBERT *is lounging lazily on the settee. There is a light in the passage. You can hear* MARGARET, *though you don't see her, just outside the room playing the violin. The door into the passage is open.*

The playing ceases. MARGARET *enters, carrying her violin. She puts her instrument in its case which has been lying open on the desk, then shuts the case. Both girls are dressed as if ready to go out.*

MARGARET   He's asleep now.

ROBERT   You see - it's done the trick.

MARGARET   (*with a bright smile*) I'm better than all your drugs, darling.

ROBERT   I should hope so. I don't want to marry a chemist's shop.

MARGARET   Idiot!

ROBERT   (*with a glance at* JOAN) Or even a chemist - if it comes to that.

JOAN   Nobody asked you, sir, she said!

MARGARET   D'you know, I'm almost sorry about this concert. I'm so afraid daddy'll wake himself up in time for the broadcast.

ROBERT   Well, it won't be for the best part of an hour.

MARGARET   An hour's sleep! It sounds so absurdly little.

JOAN   I wonder if you'll be nervous in front of the
                mike?

MARGARET   I don't suppose I'll see it. I'm playing from
                the Chancel steps.

JOAN   I wish it wasn't a sacred concert. Why don't
                you play at a profane one for a change?

MARGARET   They're not so easy to get.

ROBERT   Besides, all good musicians begin in a church.

JOAN   Oh? And where do they end?

ROBERT   In a churchyard, of course.

JOAN   (*drily*) Doesn't that rather depend on their
                doctor?

MARGARET   Well, really!

JOAN   Come along. Get your teas. (*They gather
                round a little tea table set before the hearth.*)
                I'll be mother. (*She proffers the plate of
                crumpets.*) I hope you don't mind cigarette
                ash on your crumpets.

ROBERT   (*ironically*) Not a bit.

JOAN   I've done a few without.

ROBERT   (*to* MARGARET) Which are you having?

MARGARET   Oh . . . without, I think.

ROBERT   (*as she helps herself*) Just my luck. (*As he
                takes his he blows on it, as if to free it from
                ash.*)

JOAN   Here! You're blowing butter all over me!

ROBERT   Sorry. But it just happened to have stuck to
                your ash.

MARGARET (*to* ROBERT) Robert - you don't think Daddy's seriously ill, do you?

ROBERT No. Not at present. But I think he soon may be.

JOAN What's wrong with him?

ROBERT He's on the verge of a breakdown.

MARGARET But he's always been so strong.

ROBERT When did it begin?

MARGARET Well, I suppose it must have been about the time you were home in the summer. Just before you went on this last trip.

ROBERT Do you ever remember him not being able to sleep before?

MARGARET No, never.

ROBERT He swears he's not worried about anything. Do you think that's true?

MARGARET No, I don't. I think he is worried.

ROBERT What about?

MARGARET Money.

JOAN Aren't we all?

ROBERT What makes you think he's worried about money?

MARGARET It's a silly thing to say. But I believe it's something to do with Archie.

ROBERT Archie? Oh, the boy who used to be here. I know.

MARGARET You know he came into a packet.

ROBERT I think you did tell me.

MARGARET   Well, I believe Archie's been lending Daddy
             money.

JOAN   *Archie* has?

ROBERT   But why?

MARGARET   Because he's always in and out of the house
             nowadays. And when he comes Daddy sees
             him alone in here. Never for very long.

JOAN   Perhaps the boot's on the other leg. Perhaps
             your father's been lending *him* money.

MARGARET   Daddy's not bats, darling. And then there's
             another reason.

ROBERT   What's that?

MARGARET   It's Archie's manner. He's absolutely
             unbearable sometimes. After all, it's only five
             months ago he was our shop boy.

ROBERT   How's Poppa react to him?

MARGARET   He's just very quiet. I don't like that either.
             Because he always bull-ragged him so much.
             He never liked him. We always used to feel
             sorry for Archie.

ROBERT   I'll see if I can't get your father to open out.

MARGARET   You won't do that. He's as closed as an
             oyster.

             (MRS CATT *enters. She is wearing her bonnet
             and shawl.*)

MRS CATT   Oh! Ain't you done tea yet?

MARGARET   We've just started.

ROBERT   (*drily*) And we shall be going on for quite a
             time.

MRS CATT	Only it's my afternoon off.
MARGARET	Don't wait in on our account, Mrs Catt.
MRS CATT	(*coming forward*) Well, I won't - if you don't mind. I'm feelin' that bad I can't tell yer.
JOAN	What's wrong with you today?
MRS CATT	Same as yesterday. (*To* ROBERT.) It's me nerves, sir. That's what it is. Me doctor says so. I get an awful drawn feeling across me scalp. Sort of clawing. It makes me feel as if me 'air was full of centigrades and millimetres. Though, of course, there ain't nothing there. Not so much as a nit.
ROBERT	(*assuming the professional manner*) Sounds as if you want a little electrical treatment.
MRS CATT	(*eagerly*) Oh, I Should be so grateful!
ROBERT	Take your hat off. (*He examines her head.*) Could you get your head shaved?
	(MRS CATT *starts.*)
	We must have a smooth surface to work on, you know.
MRS CATT	(*doubtfully*) I don't think my 'usband would like that. He often used ter say to me, "My girl, your 'air's your crowning glory." Of course, he *is* like that. Not so much now as 'e was. But I could ask 'im. Couldn't I? After all, there's no 'arm in asking. Is there?
ROBERT	No.
MRS CATT	No. (*She pauses.*) No. But somehow, I don't think he'd fancy me bald 'eaded.
ROBERT	Well, you ask him. You'll soon find out. Sit down. (*She does so.*) Anything else wrong?

MRS CATT   Anything else? I tell yer straight - I'm a
                walking outpatients'. And me throat tops the
                lot. I cough of a mornin' something chronic.
                (*With coyness.*) I don't 'ardly like to tell yer.

ROBERT   Let's have a look at your throat. Open your
                mouth. Say "Ah". (MRS CATT *does so - several
                times.*) That's enough. Oh, yes. You've got
                too long a uvula.

MRS CATT   (*impressed and rather pleased*) 'Ave I, sir?
                Now, isn't that interesting?

ROBERT   We'll have to nip that off. We can do that at
                the same time as the other.

MRS CATT   (*a little nervously*) Wot did you say?

ROBERT   We'll just have to cut it off. It's quite simple.
                You'll hardly feel it.

MRS CATT   Cut off my wot?

ROBERT   (*slowly and distinctly*) Your uvula.

MRS CATT   (*gaping*) My uv-u-la . . . I must remember
                that.

ROBERT   Is there anything else the matter? You're
                walking rather lame.

MARGARET   (*playing up to him*) Poor Mrs Catt suffers
                terribly from her feet, Rob. You'd better let
                the surgeon see them, too.

ROBERT   (*bending down and studying* MRS CATT's *feet*)
                Yes. Rather up-hill and down-dale, aren't
                they?

MRS CATT   Would you like me to take me shoes off?

ROBERT   Not for the present, thanks.

                (*She puts her foot forward.* ROBERT *touches
                her toes with his fingers. She winces.*)

MRS CATT   Now, go gently, young man. You 'ad a mother
                yourself, didn't yer?

ROBERT   Don't be afraid. I shan't hurt you.

MRS CATT   (*as he finds her tender spot*) Ow!

ROBERT   Sorry. That was an accident.

MRS CATT   Can't you just look at 'em without messin'
                'em about?

ROBERT   (*apparently engrossed in his observations*)
                Hm, yes. She'd probably be better without a
                toe or two. (*He presses an obvious bunion
                rather firmly.* MRS CATT *gasps.*) That one
                there, for instance.

MRS CATT   (*rising*) Thank yer, doctor. Don't think I'm
                puttin' meself forward, will yer? I'm sure you
                know wot you're talkin' about, but don't you
                worry, don't you trouble. I'll do - I'll last.
                There's plenty of others worse than me.

MARGARET   (*reproachfully*) But, Mrs Catt . . .

MRS CATT   There's nothing the matter with my feet,
                Miss, I thank yer. I can walk as well as the
                next one.

ROBERT   Don't be alarmed, Mrs Catt. It's quite a
                simple amputation. And you won't miss 'em.
                We've all got too many spare parts, you
                know.

MRS CATT   (*with a great, if slightly hysterical dignity*) If
                ever I 'as my toes touched with a knife and
                my you-know-wot cut off, it'll be done over
                my dead body. (*She moves to the door.*) I
                come into the world with me bits and pieces
                on me - such as they are - and I'm a-taking of
                'em out of it entire.

                (*She goes out, and almost instantly breaks
                into a hysterical howl.*)

JOAN   (*to* ROBERT) Now you've done it! She'll never
              forgive you.

ROBERT   Well, I shall try to survive even that.

MARGARET   She'll love you for it. You've given her
              something to chatter about for months.

              (*You can hear* MRS CATT *in the kitchen
              laughing and crying alternatively. This noise
              continues throughout the first part of the
              ensuing scene. Suddenly* AUNT MATHILDE'S
              voice is heard, endeavouring to calm her. "*Be
              quiet, be quiet! You'll wake him!*" *Then* AUNT
              MATHILDE *herself bustles in.*)

MATHILDE   (*volubly*) What is the matter with Mrs Catt?
              She came into the kitchen laughing and
              crying. And she's sitting there crying and
              laughing still. First one and then the other.

ROBERT   A little mild hysteria. It won't do her any
              harm, Aunt Mathilde. In fact, she'll feel a lot
              better as the result of it.

MATHILDE   I am not worried about Mrs Catt. (*To*
              MARGARET.) I am worried about your father,
              my love. She will wake him up and he is
              sound asleep. Can't you go to her, Robert?
              Can't you *do* something to her?

JOAN   Rob wouldn't be exactly a sedative, I'm
              afraid. He only offered to perform several
              minor operations on her -

MATHILDE   Oh - these English! They are so ungrateful.
              (*To* ROBERT, *adoringly.*) If you would only
              offer to operate on *me*! (*To* MARGARET.) You
              go, darling. Quieten her down. If need be,
              there is a bottle of cherry brandy in the
              pantry. But only if need be.

              (MARGARET *goes.*)

I am so anxious Poppa should get some rest,
Robert.

ROBERT   Margaret's been telling me some more about
him. What d'you think's wrong?

MATHILDE   Oh, he has something on his mind. Something
big. I don't know what it is. He doesn't tell
me. But he is a changed man. (*Working
herself up to a crescendo of speed.*) We have
lived together now for more than twenty
years. But he doesn't tell me a thing. I have
brought Margaret up from a baby, I have
cared for her as my own. But of course, I am
nobody. Nobody at all. I wonder he lets me
walk about the house sometimes. Nor am I
allowed to speak. I am never permitted to put
a word in sideways. Mother of God, what men
make women suffer!

                (*As she speaks*, ARCHIE *enters. He presents a
                striking metamorphosis. He is excessively
                smartly dressed. He has impertinately waited
                to uncover his head until he is well into the
                room.*)

ARCHIE   Good afternoon.

MATHILDE   (*welcoming*) Why, Archie! I didn't expect to
see you again so soon! Sit down and have
some tea. This is Archie, Robert. You
remember - he used to work here. But he is a
lucky young man. Oh, very lucky! He has
come into a great big income.

ROBERT   (*by no means unwelcoming, as he studies*
                ARCHIE) How d'you do?

ARCHIE   (*eyeing him with quiet hostility*) Do I know
you? Oh, yes. Margaret's young man.

ROBERT   (*grimly*) Margaret's young man - yes.

MATHILDE   (*volubly - to* ROBERT) Archie is a rich
            foundling now. Just like in the cinema! It is
            so good of him to come and see us still.
            Descius will be so sorry he will miss you,
            Archie. He is lying down. He has not been
            well. He's asleep.

ARCHIE   Oh? That's a pity. Because I want to see him.

ROBERT   I'm afraid you can't see him today.

ARCHIE   Who says so?

ROBERT   I say so. I happen to be looking after him.

ARCHIE   I think when he knows I'm here he'll want to
            come down. (*Nodding familiarly to* JOAN.)
            Didn't see you, Joan. How are you?

JOAN   (*acidly*) Joan's a new one on me, isn't it, Mr
            Fellowes?

ARCHIE   I don't know. I thought it was your name.

MATHILDE   (*seeing nothing in all this, laughing*) Oh, you
            are funny! He thought it was her name! You
            make me laugh, Archie. (*She has been
            pouring him out a cup of tea and now hands it
            to him.*) Now, here is a cup of tea. Help
            yourself. Make yourself at home, my dear
            boy. I must run upstairs again to Descius.

ARCHIE   Where's Margaret? She let me in, then she
            disappeared.

MATHILDE   She's looking after Mrs Catt in the kitchen.
            She has been having an attack of histrionics. I
            will tell Margaret you would like to see her.
            That will make her hurry.

            (*She bustles out.*)

ROBERT   (*between his teeth*) I don't think it matters all
            that much.

ARCHIE   (*lounging insolently against the desk*) Are you
              trying to be offensive or what?

ROBERT   (*quietly*) If I were, you'd know it.

              (*There is a pause.* ARCHIE *begins to whistle
              Solveig's song from "Peer Gynt" slowly and
              insistently. The tension between the two men
              is very marked.* JOAN *rises quickly. She
              gathers the tea things onto the tray.*)

JOAN   (*to* ARCHIE, *interrupting his melody*) Aren't
              you going to drink your tea?

              (ARCHIE *shakes his head.*)

              Then I think I'll take the tray.

              (*She takes up the tray, leaving the little
              folding table upon which it has been standing.
              As she passes* ARCHIE *he places his untouched
              cup and saucer on it. Then he impudently
              touches and feels the material of* JOAN'S
              dress.)

ARCHIE   Nice stuff.

              (JOAN *draws away from him with repugnance
              and departs quickly with the tray.* ARCHIE *goes
              on with his whistling.* ROBERT *has filled his
              pipe and strikes a match to light it.
              Simultaneously* ARCHIE *takes a cigarette from
              his case. He crosses and lights the cigarette
              from* ROBERT'S *match, after which he pointedly
              blows out the match and moves across to the
              desk, still whistling.* ROBERT'S *face is a study.*)

              You're a medicine man, aren't you?

ROBERT   If you must know. Ship's doctor - Merchant
              service.

ARCHIE   Aha. What's the matter with the old man?

ROBERT   He's getting on, you know.

ARCHIE   (*with a glance*) Is that all?

ROBERT   (*shrugging*) My opinion.

ARCHIE   Pity. D'you like him?

ROBERT   Yep.

ARCHIE   Know anything about him?

ROBERT   That's my business.

ARCHIE   I was only asking. (*He picks up a small object from the desk and examines it critically.*) Hullo! What's this? Haven't seen this before.

ROBERT   (*grudgingly*) It's an old Japanese netsuki - a carved ivory button.

ARCHIE   (*with a slow smile*) Where did the old devil scrounge it, I wonder?

ROBERT   If you must know, I've just brought it home from Kobe.

ARCHIE   (*still studying it*) Mice on a clam shell. Prettily done. It's for sale, I suppose?

ROBERT   I expect so.

ARCHIE   (*airily*) I think I'll have it. How much?

ROBERT   Can't help you.

ARCHIE   I'll take it, anyhow. Tell the old man to chalk it up.

ROBERT   (*sharply*) It's not *my* shop!

ARCHIE   (*casually slipping the netsuki into his pocket*) Oh, very well.

ROBERT   Do you mind putting that back?

              (*He takes a step towards* ARCHIE, *who turns on him like a rat.*)

ARCHIE You keep your hands off me! Just because I used to serve behind that blasted counter in there, you think I'm nobody, don't you? I'll have to teach you different.

(*He turns scornfully away.* ROBERT *takes him firmly by the back, pinioning him by the arms. He inserts his hand into the youth's pocket and withdraws the netsuki.*)

ROBERT That's kind of you. And here endeth the *first* lesson.

(ROBERT *lays the netsuki down on the little table.* ARCHIE *shakes his coat into position, like a terrier. There is a short pause.*)

ARCHIE (*with an ugly nonchalance*) You're going to marry into this family, aren't you?

ROBERT That is the idea.

ARCHIE Then I shouldn't advise you to make an enemy of me.

ROBERT (*with anger*) Who do you think you are?

ARCHIE (*coolly*) Just myself.

ROBERT And what the hell are you doing snooping around here and behaving like a shoddy little gangster?

ARCHIE Bad vice - curiosity.

ROBERT Well, so long as I'm here you're going to mend your manners, see?

ARCHIE (*smiling*) Or Captain Bligh'll treat me to a dose of the quarter deck, I suppose?

ROBERT You've said it.

ARCHIE 'Fraid I'm not impressed.

(MARGARET *enters*.)

Hullo, Margaret! Going to broadcast tonight, I see.

MARGARET   Yes. From St Peter's.

ARCHIE   Pity I shan't hear you. (*With one eye on* ROBERT *he sidles up to her*.) But I've got some seats for Covent Garden on Wednesday.

MARGARET   Oh, the "Meistersingers"? Really?

ARCHIE   Like to come with me?

MARGARET   (*hardly knowing how to take this*) No, I'm afraid I can't manage Wednesday.

ARCHIE   Why not? We might have a bite somewhere afterwards. Cafe Royal - The Trocadero. I don't give a damn.

MARGARET   No, I'm afraid I can't.

ARCHIE   (*with a glance at* ROBERT) Why not? Won't your young man release you?

ROBERT   It's been a date for a long time.

ARCHIE   (*airily*) Think it over.

ROBERT   (*quietly*) I don't see the necessity.

ARCHIE   (*to* ROBERT) I didn't ask you to butt in, did I?

             (*For answer* ARCHIE *gets a quick upper thrust which lands him on the carpet. He scrambles into a sitting posture, his hands to his jaw*.)

MARGARET   Rob! Be careful! Don't!

             (ARCHIE *gets up. He takes a step or two backwards and holds a revolver -* DESCIUS' *revolver - in his hand. He is white with venom*.)

ROBERT   Oh? Got a sting, have you?

MARGARET   Archie! Put that down!

ARCHIE   (*to* ROBERT) If you touch me again I'll let
              daylight into you.

              (JOAN *returns. She remains at the top of the
              steps.*)

JOAN   My goodness! I seem to have missed
              something!

              (ARCHIE *slips the revolver back into his hip
              pocket rather furtively, as though he realises
              he has made a mistake. He takes up his hat.*)

ARCHIE   No, Joan. You haven't missed anything. Not a
              single thing.

              (*He goes up the steps to the door.*)

              So long, everybody.

              (*He makes a clicking noise with his tongue as
              he passes* JOAN *and goes out. A moment later
              the door slams.* JOAN *comes down into the
              room.*)

JOAN   Well, well, well!

MARGARET   It's incredible! It's absolutely incredible!

JOAN   What's the little swine doing with a revolver?

MARGARET   I haven't a notion! He's utterly irresponsible.

ROBERT   Oh, no. He's not.

MARGARET   But, listen. Supposing we're right, supposing
              he is financing Daddy - well, you don't
              usually lend money at the point of a pistol, do
              you?

JOAN   No. But you might try to get it back that way.

ROBERT   I think he's a creditor trying to collect.
                Nothing else fits in.

MARGARET   Well he won't be back today, thank goodness.
                That's one comfort.

ROBERT   And I doubt if he'll be back tomorrow, either.
                I fancy he may be nursing a swollen jaw.

JOAN   I see! That accounts for the pistol.

ROBERT   (*with a grin*) I think I should have spared his
                beauty if I'd known he could draw on me. But
                I didn't.

JOAN   Good!

MARGARET   (*going to the violin case and fastening it*)
                Don't let's talk any more about it. Or my
                playing'll be like nothing on God's earth. It's
                time we were off. Joan darling, put away that
                little table, will you?

ROBERT   I will.

                (JOAN *picks up the little netsuki from the table
                and lays it on a tiny Persian tray standing on
                the mantelpiece. She folds up the table and
                stands it in a corner.* DESCIUS *enters. He looks
                older and worn.*)

MARGARET   (*in some distress*) Daddy! You were fast
                asleep! This is frightfully naughty of you.

DESCIUS   I've had my nap. I've had my forty winks.

MARGARET   But it's so little, and you need such a lot.

DESCIUS   Did you think I was going to miss your
                broadcast? My little girl on the air? Oh, no,
                no, no. It means too much.

ROBERT   Your doctor says you'd have done better to
                miss it.

DESCIUS   My doctor does not know everything.

ROBERT   (*significantly*) No. And I think he could help
               you more if he did.

DESCIUS   (*with a flash of asperity*) Don't be a fool,
               Robert. (*Then quietly again.*) What is there to
               know? I have lost the power of sleeping. That
               is all. It does happen. There is nothing to
               worry about. It will come back. One day.

JOAN   I think you ought to go away for a good long
               rest.

DESCIUS   (*eyeing her*) Oh? Do you?

JOAN   Torquay or somewhere like that.

ROBERT   Cairo's a nice place in the winter.

DESCIUS   Cairo! I've called in the wrong doctor,
               Margaret. Cairo! A poor old antique dealer.

JOAN   (*with dry insistence*) There's still Torquay.

ROBERT   That would be better than nothing.

DESCIUS   It's not possible. Business is difficult. I can't
               leave it. My new boy is a young fool. Aunt
               Mathilde is an old goose. Mrs Catt, I suppose,
               could take over.

MARGARET   Mrs Catt? Daddy, do be sensible.

DESCIUS   (*rather pathetically*) I was only making some
               silly little fun, darling. But you can't joke
               cleverly when you're very tired.

MARGARET   Oh, my dear . . . (*She kisses* DESCIUS.)

JOAN   (*casually*) A pity Archie isn't still here. He
               could have managed for you.

               (*The mention of* ARCHIE *causes* DESCIUS *to
               react - very slightly, but perceptibly. They are*

now watching him intently. Aware that they are doing so, DESCIUS *is on his guard.*)

DESCIUS   Yes. Archie is a very clever boy. I'm afraid I underrated his abilities while he was with me.

MARGARET   He called to see you this afternoon.

DESCIUS   (*sharply*) Archie? Did he? Did he go away?

MARGARET   Yes, when he heard you were lying down.

ROBERT   And I don't think he'll be back for a day or two.

DESCIUS   (*quite master of himself again*) Oh well, that's a pity. Why, I might have asked him if he could come back for a little while and take charge so that I could go to - Torquay, was it?

JOAN   Torquay.

DESCIUS   Torquay - yes. (*Casually.*) Oh well when he calls again perhaps we can arrange it.

           (*He deliberately breaks the conversation by picking up from the top of the radio, where they have been lying, the blowpipe and the box of darts from the preceding scene.*)

           Robert, I have never sold your blowpipe. No one is interested. Or perhaps we are asking too much money for it. All your other things have gone. Even your Birmingham Buddha - I sold it to a Bishop.

MARGARET   And I've had my cheque!

ROBERT   Then I think the blowpipe ought to be yours.

DESCIUS   Well, we will work it that way, if you like.

ROBERT   (*significantly*) Only be careful, my friend. Be very careful.

DESCIUS   (*to* ROBERT) You may take charge of it, if
               you're afraid. Here is the inventory. One
               blowpipe. (*Opening the little box.*) Two darts.

ROBERT   Don't be silly.

DESCIUS   I'm not at all silly. That's what you *were*
               thinking.

JOAN   Well, unless you're going to miss your
               concert -

MARGARET   We can still make it comfortably. (*She kisses*
               DESCIUS.) Good bye, darling.

DESCIUS   And play well, my sweetheart. I shall be
               listening. (*Taking a cigar.*) I shall smoke a
               cigar and sit and wait for the time when I
               shall hear you coming out of the nothing in
               my little room.

ROBERT   (*producing a penknife*) Knife?

DESCIUS   (*piercing his cigar with a match*) Thank you,
               Robert, no. I prefer a match. It is the best way
               to pierce a cigar. the one thing you mustn't do
               to a good cigar is to bite it. I'm always telling
               my American friends that.

MARGARET   (*as they go to the door*) We shan't be back till
               after midnight.

DESCIUS   Oh, it's a long service!

MARGARET   Rob's taking us out to supper afterwards at
               the Corner House.

JOAN   We're going to see life!

ROBERT   Let's see if we can get a cab.

MARGARET   (*to* DESCIUS) Shall I turn the radio on for you?

DESCIUS   Yes - not too loud.

(MARGARET *switches on the radio. Some very soft music comes through.*)

MARGARET   (*to* DESCIUS) Goodnight, Daddy.

DESCIUS   Good bye, my darling - good luck.

MARGARET   (*she is on the stairs; she stops, comes down again and puts her violin on the stool*) Do you know I'm very cross with you?

DESCIUS   Why? What have I done?

MARGARET   It's what you haven't.

DESCIUS   Oh! A sin of omission! They are always the worst.

MARGARET   You don't seem to be trying to get well.

DESCIUS   Don't I? Sometimes at my age one does wonder whether it is worth all the trouble.

MARGARET   You selfish old thing!

DESCIUS   Selfish?

MARGARET   What do you think would happen to me if anything happened to you?

DESCIUS   You've got Robert.

MARGARET   That's quite a different thing. I love Robert, I'm a part of you.

DESCIUS   Oh! I am going up in the world. I didn't know I was quite so important.

MARGARET   Oh, Daddy! You'll break my heart. (*Kneeling beside him.*) I love you. It's quite different from the way I love Rob. If he died, the world would go all dark. But if you died, there wouldn't be a world at all. I'm making a fool of myself, I know. Please forgive me, but I'm worried about you. I'm desperate! You must get well . . . (*She drops her head on his knee - he kisses her hair.*)

DESCIUS   Oh - so that is an order, is it?

MARGARET   Indeed it is.

DESCIUS   Well, here we execute all orders with
               promptness and despatch. The customer is
               always right.

MARGARET   I wish you wouldn't joke.

DESCIUS   I'm not joking. You want me to get well. I
               will get well.

MARGARET   Is that a promise?

DESCIUS   That is a promise. And I always keep my
               promises.

MARGARET   Darling, let's seal it. Shall we?

DESCIUS   Seal it! How?

MARGARET   Honour bright. (*Drawing her hand across her
               throat.*) Like that.

DESCIUS   (*repeating her action*) Honour bright.
               Satisfied? (*He holds his hand out - she takes
               it. He kisses her hand. She kisses him on the
               cheek.*)

MARGARET   Yes.

               (*She takes up her violin and goes. In the
               passage* MARGARET *and* AUNT MATHILDE *can be
               heard speaking.*)

DESCIUS   (*dropping his head on to his hand with a deep
               groan*) Honour bright.

               (AUNT MATHILDE *enters.*)

MATHILDE   Descius! Are you down? Are you up?

DESCIUS   (*looking at her*) Make up your mind which
               you mean.

MATHILDE   Why can't you do as you're told? Robert sent
              you to lie down. Margaret sent you to sleep.
              And now, in half a minute, here you are fast
              awake. What is the good of it all? I am sick
              and tired of it! I am . . . (*Seeing the tragedy
              in his face*.) . . . Descius! What is the matter?
              Don't look at me like that! What is the
              matter?

DESCIUS   Don't worry, Mathilde. (*He rises and moves
              to the radio.*) Don't worry, I would tell you if
              only you were more trustworthy.

              (DESCIUS *switches off the radio, and sits at his
              desk.*)

MATHILDE   (*with real emotion*) If I were trustworthy!
              Mother of God! Here we have shared our lives
              together for twenty years! I have slaved for
              you and the little one if ever a woman did!
              Tell me - accuse me - yes! Please accuse me
              if I have ever been disloyal to you, if I have
              ever chattered when I should have held tight
              to my tongue, if I have ever thought of myself
              - even once - at your expense or at Margaret's
              expense or at the expense of the business
              which is our life's blood! Accuse me! Accuse
              me! You can't! And yet you say I am not
              trustworthy.

DESCIUS   (*with contrition*) I am sorry, Mathilde. I am a
              sick man . . . impatient. You must forgive me.
              One says things one doesn't mean, you know.

MATHILDE   What is it that's destroying you? For it is
              destroying you! Tell me. Tell old Mathilde.
              Your little sister was. (*Putting her arms
              around him.*) She is still your little sister,
              poor old woman.

DESCIUS   I am in terrible trouble. I don't know where to
              turn.

MATHILDE   (*in an awed tone*) Descius! It's not the police?
                (*And we realise at once that she is no stranger
                to his profession.*) They've not found out?

DESCIUS   No.

MATHILDE   You've not been given away? Oh, God!

DESCIUS   No no no no! It's worse than the police.

MATHILDE   Worse than the police! But that's impossible!
                In our position nothing could be worse than
                the police! (*Her voice rising hysterically,*
                DESCIUS *hushes her.*) I am sorry I get so
                excited. It upsets you, I know. But I will
                control myself. I will be quiet. Tell me. Tell
                me, quite calmly.

DESCIUS   (*leaning forward*) Very well.

                (*There is a sudden sharp knocking at the
                street door.* AUNT MATHILDE *rises with a little
                scream.*)

MATHILDE   Oh!

DESCIUS   Sssh! Don't be alarmed. Nothing is going to
                happen Quickly. (*Another knock.*) Why
                doesn't that old fool woman answer the door?

MATHILDE   Oh, of course! She must have gone home. I
                will go.

                (*She goes. After a moment voices can be
                heard in the passage.* DESCIUS *listens intently
                and with relief.*)

MORRIS   (*off*) Good Evening, Miss Mathilde. Is Mr
                Heiss in?

MATHILDE   (*off*) Yes, come in, Morris. He is not very well.

                (AUNT MATHILDE *returns.*)

                It's Morris, Descius. He has something for
                you.

(CORDER MORRIS *enters. He is in a rather*
happy mood. He is dressed all in black with a
black billycock hat. He carries a small black
Gladstone bag. AUNT MATHILDE *follows him*
in.)

MORRIS   Good evening, Mr Heiss.

DESCIUS   Come in, Morris, come in.

MORRIS   Sorry to disturb a pleasant Sunday afternoon.

DESCIUS   What are Sunday afternoons for, except to pay
            visits to one's friends?

MORRIS   (*putting down his bag on the desk*) I've
            something here won't keep.

DESCIUS   (*laconically*) Eh?

MORRIS   At least I don't want to keep it.

DESCIUS   Mathilde! Get me a newspaper.

            (*She produces a newspaper and spreads it on*
            the desk.)

            What's it this time?

MORRIS   Gold.

DESCIUS   (*his eyes bright*) Gold? Ha!

MORRIS   Quite a lot of it. And all eighteen carat.

            (*During what follows he produces the*
            contents of his bag. It consists of some solid
            gold boxes, some gold bottle tops and a good
            deal of smashed, twisted and hammered gold
            which has been the backs of brushes, combs
            and mirrors.)

DESCIUS   (*with a slow smile*) And who's been unlucky
            this time?

MORRIS	(*smiling, too*) Nobody alive.
DESCIUS	(*there is a shadow of hesitation in his voice*) Nobody alive?
MATHILDE	Descius, don't touch it!
DESCIUS	(*silencing her*) Tch, tch, tch!
MORRIS	(*cheerily*) Don't worry, Miss Mathilde. I haven't put anyone to sleep.
DESCIUS	(*examining the gold*) Oh, a gold toilet set! Aha! Yes! Very fine.
MORRIS	Only the metal. I've wrenched off the brushes and combs and destroyed 'em. And the bottles, too. I've even smashed the mirrors. (*Laughing at his on temerity.*) Look. There's a couple of solid gold trinket boxes. Weighty.
DESCIUS	Where did this come from?
MORRIS	Lady Brenzett's. South Audley Street.
MATHILDE	Didn't I read somewhere she had died just the other day?
MORRIS	You did. Friday. (*With a chuckle.*) My God, Heiss, it's the slickest job o' work ever I did! And the simplest. I called there this morning, all in black. I wore glasses - pince-nez. I said I was from the undertakers. It was Sunday so they couldn't have checked up on me even if they'd been suspicious. But they weren't. I said there were some final measurements wanted. Would I come in? Would I come in! (*He roars with laughter.*) They took me upstairs to the bedroom, left me on my own for only-o two whole minutes if you please, and my little black bag came out fuller than when it when in. (*Patting the bag.*) What d'yer think, eh? Wasn't that rich? I've not done laughing yet!

DESCIUS   (*with a connoisseur's smile*) It is almost
               French.

MATHILDE   And I suppose she was laid out on her bed all
               the time?

MORRIS   She was.

MATHILDE   Think of her feelings!

MORRIS   (*slyly*) I reckon the old dame saw the joke.
               For I rather fancy I caught her smiling at me!

MATHILDE   Oh! (*She moves to the couch, shaking her
               head, half amused, half shocked.*)

MORRIS   (*to* DESCIUS) Now, listen. None of your twenty
               five per cents on this. 'Cos it's all eighteen
               carat. Solid, saleable stuff.

DESCIUS   Very well. I'll tell you what we do. We'll go
               fifty-fifty.

MORRIS   Fifty- fifty! You *are* in a generous mood!

DESCIUS   The truth is, I have a favour to ask you.

MORRIS   Oh?

DESCIUS   Yes, and something not very pleasant to tell
               you. I was beginning to tell Mathilde here
               when you knocked.

MORRIS   What are you getting at?

DESCIUS   Do you remember last August coming here
               and my paying you for that Porchester Place
               stuff? It was in the evening. You were all out
               at theatre, Mathilde.

MATHILDE   At the theatre? Were we? Oh yes, I remember.

MORRIS   Well?

DESCIUS   We had a heart to heart talk, I fancy.

MORRIS   We certainly did.

DESCIUS   Do you remember, at the end of our interview,
              you tapped this suit of armour? You hoped
              there wasn't a nark inside.

MORRIS   Very likely.

DESCIUS   (*pointing to the other suit*) Why didn't you
              tap that one? Why? Why? (*He pauses.*) Do
              you know who was behind it? My damned
              boy! (*He brings his clenched fist down on the
              desk*)

MATHILDE   Archie?

DESCIUS   (*grimly*) Archie.

MORRIS   That young Fellowes? You mean he
              overheard?

DESCIUS   He has been blackmailing me ever since.

MATHILDE   Archie!

MORRIS   Archie Fellowes . . . I've seen him about the
              West End quite a lot lately. I thought you told
              me he'd come into money.

DESCIUS   He has come into money. My money!

MATHILDE   Oh, that villainous boy! So that is why he is
              always haunting us!

MORRIS   Got a neat little flatlet in Jermyn Street,
              hasn't he?

DESCIUS   (*he comes between them*) A flatlet in Jermyn
              Street? He might have a suite at the Ritz on
              what he's had out of me. Oh, I know it all
              sounds very funny. But it is tearing me to
              pieces.

MATHILDE   How often have I told you I distrusted
              Archie? He was always insolent - he was
              selfish, he was cruel! Why did you not listen

to me when I told you over and over again to
get rid of him?

DESCIUS (*ignoring this feminine injustice*) He has had
five thousand pounds out of me.

MATHILDE (*in horror*) Five thousand pounds!

DESCIUS In less than five months. It never stops. It
never stops. He has no mercy, no pity. He is
slowly bleeding me to death.

MORRIS And you've knuckled down? Pretty hot laws
against blackmail, you know.

DESCIUS The law does not protect me. I live outside it.

MORRIS Can't you call his bluff? He daren't go to the
police.

DESCIUS The police? Of course he won't go to the
police. No - it is something much more subtle
than that.

MATHILDE What is it?

DESCIUS He threatens to tell Margaret. You see, he has
found my Achilles' heel. (*He sinks down on
the stool.*)

MATHILDE Margaret!

MORRIS Your daughter?

DESCIUS I have brought her up to believe in me as an
honest man. She adores me. It is a perfect
relationship.

MATHILDE (*in great distress*) Margaret!

DESCIUS If she should discover that I am . . . what I
am. Worse than a thief. A fence. Worse than
that. A man who has been found guilty of
murder.

MATHILDE (*wailing*) Oh! Oh!

DESCIUS   A murderer. Well, I do not know whether I
           am or not. It was so dark. Besides, there were
           too many of us. But a convict, with the scars
           of the lash on my back. I am that, at least.
           And he would do it. He would tell her. He
           would not hesitate. And, he would enjoy
           doing it.

MATHILDE   Margaret - no, of course, she must not know.

MORRIS   (*cynically*) Gee! It just shows what a
           dangerous thing honesty can be in a family.

DESCIUS   It just shows that, once a man has tuned his
           back on a community, he can never turn his
           face to it again. (*Rising.*) Now, I want your
           help, Morris. I shall have to bolt. I must get
           to America.

MATHILDE   (*in amazement*) America!

DESCIUS   In England sooner or later Archie will always
           find me.

MATHILDE   But what is to become of us?

DESCIUS   You and Margaret must follow me. We will
           tell her it is necessary for my health.

MATHILDE   But she's going to marry Robert!

DESCIUS   Well! He can get transferred to a trans
           Atlantic line, can't he? A wife in New York -
           see? (*He is now behind the desk.*) Now, for
           the time being, I must be ill. I must go to -
           where was it - Torquay - for a good long
           holiday. That will throw sand in Archie's
           eyes. Meanwhile the shop must be kept open.
           More sand! But I shall *not* go to Torquay. I
           shall sail for New York. (*To* MORRIS.) Now,
           you know New York. (*Significantly.*) Our part
           of New York. I must keep the pot boiling.
           And to do that I must have my . . . contacts.

MORRIS   Sure. I'll fix it.

DESCIUS   Thank you, Morris. Thank you.

MORRIS   (*rising with electrifying vehemence*) Hey! I've
                just thought of something! (*To* DESCIUS.) If
                Archie knows all about *you*, he must know a
                hell of a lot about ME!

DESCIUS   (*drily*) Yes, I thought you would see that
                before we had finished.

MORRIS   But this is serious! This is bloody serious.
                We've got to do something about it. (*Grimly.*)
                Look, Heiss. Cut out this flight-into-Egypt
                business. There's only one thing we've got to
                do. We've got to take him for a ride.

DESCIUS   (*quickly*) No. Oh, no.

MATHILDE   (*in a whisper*) Kill . . . ? (*She rises.*)

MORRIS   Listen. I'm not living in the same world with
                a blackmailer who has anything on me.

DESCIUS   (*slowly*) Do you think I haven't thought of it?

MORRIS   I know where he lives. If he's wise to me,
                I'll put two of the boys on to him.

MATHILDE   No no no!

MORRIS   What d'you reckon his life's worth, Miss
                Mathilde? I'd think no more of killing him
                than I would of killing a rat.

DESCIUS   (*quietly, firmly*) No.

MORRIS   Heiss, don't tell me you're yellow.

DESCIUS   (*with dignity*) Yes, I *am* yellow - when it
                comes to that.

MORRIS   You can put too big a value on human life,
                y'know.

DESCIUS   You forget - I've been through it - all.

MORRIS   Well, he'd better lookout with me - when
                   you're gone.

DESCIUS   That is your business. (*Holding out his hand
                   with finality.*) Good night.

MORRIS   (*taking it*) Good night. Good night, Miss
                   Mathilde.

                   (MORRIS *goes out, closing the room door after
                   him. A moment later, the front door slams
                   behind him.*)

MATHILDE   (*wailing*) Oh, Descius! This is terrible! All we
                   have worked for wrecked - wrecked!

DESCIUS   You mustn't give way, Mathilde. You must
                   help me. Bring me the big crucible.

                   (*She fetches a large crucible from the
                   cupboard below the sink and sets it on the
                   desk.* DESCIUS, *using the newspaper as a sort
                   of funnel, lets the gold articles slide into the
                   crucible.*)

                   If I am to bolt, all this stuff must be melted
                   down at once - tonight! Open the furnace
                   door.

                   (AUNT MATHILDE *goes to the mantelpiece, but
                   before she turns the spring*, MRS CATT *is
                   heard in the passage singing raucously.*)

                   No! Wait!

                   (*He rushes across the room with the crucible
                   and just succeeds in putting it in the cupboard
                   below the sink when the door flies open and*
                   MRS CATT *appears. Her bonnet and shawl are
                   awry, her face pink and beaming. In her hand
                   is an empty bottle which has contained cherry
                   brandy. She is gloriously drunk and is singing*

> *at the top of her voice, in a tune fairly*
> *reminiscent of "The Red River Valley".)*

MRS CATT   They say there's a barge on the river-
              They say that it's loaded with beer!

MATHILDE   (*in nervousness and amazement*) Where've
              you been?

MRS CATT   (*swaying*) Under the table in the kitchen. I've
              had a beautiful snooze.

DESCIUS   You're drunk.

MRS CATT   (*with dignity*) Hush. (*Somehow she descends
              the stairs. She comes to them holding out the
              bottle.*) Where's this belong?

MATHILDE   (*seizing it*) Mother of God! My cherry brandy!
              Why, it's empty! (*Regarding her.*) You
              haven't? You have! You'll die, stupid.

MRS CATT   (*coyly, wagging a finger*) No. Never say die!
              Never felt better in me life. Never felt more
              alive! It's a wonderful feeling! I must get
              home to the old man before it wears off! Hip!
              Hark at me! Don't come to door. No trouble.
              See meself out. Goo' night, Miss Mathilde.
              Goo' night, Mr Heiss.

              They say there's a barge on the river
              They say that it's loaded with beer!
              They say there's a barge on the river,
              Gorblimey! I wish it was 'ere!

              (*She sways happily out of sight along the
              passage.*)

MATHILDE   (*crushed*) A bottle of the best cherry brandy.
              A whole bottle. The very best. I can't stand
              any more, Descius. I'm going upstairs.

DESCIUS   Why, you are all worn out, Mathilde. Go
              upstairs and lie down. I turn out the lights.
              Then I come.

(*She goes. He turns out the main light. The
room is now lit by the lamp on the desk and
the glow from the electric stove.* DESCIUS
*stands for a moment in deep thought. Then his
sharp eye falls on* MORRIS's *little black bag
which he has left on the desk.*)

(*angrily*) Fool! He has left his bag! (*He
considers a moment.*) Better put it in the shop.

(*He goes out into the dark shop and switches
on the light. A moment later, along the
lighted passageway, comes* ARCHIE. *He walks
into the room, takes off his hat and overcoat.
Then he goes up to the mantelpiece and snubs
his cigarette out. His glance falls on the little
Japanese netsuki lying on the tray. He picks it
up, laughs softly, throws it into the air,
catches it light-heartedly and slips it into his
pocket.*)

ARCHIE   (*slyly*) One in the eye for you, Mr Robert.

(*He has hardly done so when* DESCIUS *switches
off the light in the shop and returns. He sees
there is somebody in the room, but it is a
moment before he recognises who it is.*)

DESCIUS   (*slowly, hollowly*) You . . .

ARCHIE   Not very wise, is it, to leave your street door
                 open - even if you have got a drunken
                 servant! It's all right. I've shut it now.

DESCIUS   I didn't expect to see you again quite so soon.

ARCHIE   Ha! I've been doing a spot of racing. Don't
                 worry. I'm not going to do any more. But I
                 need a couple of hundred.

DESCIUS   A couple of hundred!

ARCHIE   That's all - for the present.

DESCIUS   I! To be bled for a couple of hundred! To pay
             some beastly bookmaker! I - who have never
             gambled, not once in all my life!

ARCHIE   No, you always bet on certainties. (*Slyly*.) But
             you do take your risks, don't you?

             (DESCIUS *takes a step towards him.* ARCHIE
             *produces his revolver, just turning it back and
             forth in his hands as if examining it*.)

DESCIUS   You filthy parasite!

ARCHIE   Big fleas have little fleas upon their backs to
             bite 'em. I'm not quite clear of risks, am I?

DESCIUS   (*with a forlorn shrug*) This is the last you get
             from me.

ARCHIE   Till next time.

DESCIUS   This is the last you get from me, Archie. I am
             a very sick man. You are killing me by
             inches. My heart has given way under the
             worry. I have angina. I am to go away for a
             long holiday. (ARCHIE *laughs*.) Oh, yes! You
             may laugh, but you are killing the goose that
             lays the golden eggs. Archie, listen. Can't we
             come to some arrangement about this? I've
             paid very dearly for my - indiscretion.

ARCHIE   Nothing'd suit me better. What's your idea - a
             lump sum?

DESCIUS   That would only be possible . . . if I could
             trust you.

ARCHIE   That's a pity. Because I think we could be
             more useful to each other as . . . friends.

DESCIUS   Did you say "friends"?

ARCHIE   Shall I say "partners"?

DESCIUS   What, precisely, do you mean?

ARCHIE   I know this can't go on - just as you do. Let's
                bury the hatchet, shall we? (*He puts the
                revolver in his pocket.*)

DESCIUS   With all my heart.

ARCHIE   I'll admit I'm sorry for you. I never liked
                you, but I'm sorry for you. And I like your
                family - one member of it.

DESCIUS   (*now sitting at his desk*) Ho! Aunt Mathilde!
                Yes, she was always kind to you.

ARCHIE   Margaret. (*There is a long pause.* ARCHIE'S
                hand goes up to his tender jaw.) It would be
                rather fun to marry Margaret.

DESCIUS   (*his face is inscrutable*) Margaret is engaged.

ARCHIE   Engagements can be broken off. I don't think
                it's likely to be a happy marriage - hers and
                Robert's.

DESCIUS   (*moistening his lips*) Why not?

ARCHIE   When Robert finds out - he *may* find out -
                what you really are, d'you think he's quite the
                sort to stick by her? He's a bit English, you
                know. We've funny ideas about these things -
                in England - some of us.

DESCIUS   I'm still waiting for your - proposition.

ARCHIE   You've a lot of influence with Margaret.
                Almost an unnatural influence. Haven't you?
                Get her to break with Robert. You can do it.
                Then how about me for a son-in-law? And a
                partner? At least you'll be spending your
                money in your family.

DESCIUS   Does Margaret like you?

ARCHIE   She likes me quite a lot. Only she doesn't
          know it. I could easily make her like me
          more. She's very simple, you know.

          (ARCHIE *turns leisurely to sit on the settee.*
          DESCIUS *turns. His glance falls on the*
          blowpipe and darts on the radio cabinet.
          There is a long pause. By the expression on
          DESCIUS' *face, it is clear that* ARCHIE'S *doom*
          is sealed.)

DESCIUS   I suppose it might be possible. I'll have to
          think it over. (*A clock chimes the half hour.*)
          Half past six. Just time for Margaret's
          broadcast. (*He takes the blowpipe and darts*
          from the cabinet and turns on the radio with
          his other hand.) If you are in love with her,
          you will like it, Archie. She is broadcasting
          from a church - a religious service. Evensong.
          (*The sound of* MARGARET *playing an "Ave*
          Maria" comes through the radio.) A cigar,
          Archie?

ARCHIE   I never eat or drink in your house. I don't
          think I'd better smoke one of your cigars.

DESCIUS   (*pleasantly*) Ah, you think of everything,
          Archie. Well, while we're listening, I'll
          consider your proposition a little further.

ARCHIE   Take your time.

          (DESCIUS *has the blowpipe in his fingers. From*
          where ARCHIE *sits it must look extremely like*
          a cigar. The old man carefully inserts one of
          the darts, which merely looks as though he is
          piercing his smoke. He raises it softly to his
          lips. ARCHIE *is now not looking directly at*
          him, but is listening to the music. DESCIUS
          blows. ARCHIE *starts and looks around.*
          DESCIUS *is watching him eagerly.*)

ARCHIE   (*sharply*) What's that?

DESCIUS   What's what?

ARCHIE   Thought I heard something drop.

DESCIUS   I didn't hear anything. (*And he knows he has missed. He lays down the blowpipe and rises, taking his keys from a drawer and going to the safe.*) Oh, I was forgetting. (*He opens the safe and counts out some notes.*) A couple of hundred, I think you said?

ARCHIE   That's right.

DESCIUS   (*drily*) Well, in case either of us should forget, perhaps you'd better have them now.

                (*The old man comes forward, the notes in his hand. Suddenly he appears seized with a heart attack. He grips his left breast and falls back in the armchair. The notes flutter to the floor.*)

DESCIUS   (*with a deep groan*) Oh, that pain again! Archie! Archie - I'm going . . .

                (ARCHIE *springs up, revolver in hand, and crosses to him. He bends over his victim.*)

ARCHIE   What is it? What can I do?

DESCIUS   (*feebly*) The drops - a small bottle - the desk drawer.

                (ARCHIE *rushes to the desk, lays down his revolver and rummages hurriedly in the centre drawer. His search is unsuccessful. He returns to* DESCIUS *who is lying back with his eyes closed. He bends over him again.*)

ARCHIE   They're not there. Can't you - can't you tell me where they are, Guv? (*He shakes* DESCIUS, *now more thoroughly alarmed.*) Guv! Where are they?

(The old man opens his eyes. They are bright, healthy and glittering. His right arm shoots up and he seizes the youth by the throat. He rises, and they sway backwards and forwards in a soundless death struggle. All the while the magnificent music goes on. Then suddenly ARCHIE *frees himself sufficiently to give a piercing scream for help.* DESCIUS *clasps one hand across his mouth and stops the cry. Gradually* ARCHIE *weakens.* DESCIUS *forces him backwards over the central stool. He lies there with* DESCIUS *standing above him still gripping his throat. It is some while before* DESCIUS *releases his grip and steps back, surveying the horror of what he has done.* ARCHIE *is quite still. At the same moment, the music begins to fade. There is a pause. Then* AUNT MATHILDE *enters.)*

MATHILDE   Descius!

(He turns to her and she sees the body.)

What have you done?

(He does not answer at once, and she gives a sharp little scream of fear.)

DESCIUS   Shhhh!

(She comes forward and touches ARCHIE'S *arm. At her touch the body turns slightly and crashes to the floor, face down. She kneels beside it, crossing herself. Suddenly from the radio, a fine moving voice - a priest's voice - is heard praying at the church service.)*

VOICE   "Lighten our darkness, we beseech Thee, O Lord, and by Thy great mercy defend us from all perils and dangers of this night . . ."

(The lights slowly start to fade on the word "mercy" and the music on the radio swells to forte as the lights fade to black.)

ACT THREE

It is about ten o'clock the following Tuesday morning, a fine, clear, bright wintry day.

Sitting on the desk, reading a newspaper, is STEVE HUBBARD, ARCHIE'S *successor as shop assistant. He is a pink-faced boy of about sixteen with chestnut hair and a green baize apron. He has a feather duster under one arm.* MRS CATT, *melancholy and bilious, is gingerly doing the honours of cleanliness to the floor with a dustpan and brush in front of the settee.*

STEVE   (*reading aloud*) "Mrs Towser, of Dunmow, who passed close to the spot where the body was found, has informed the police that she saw a red car standing at the side of the road about 10.45 p.m. on Sunday. She does not know what make of car it was. Only its rear light was burning. The number plate had been obscured by a green silk handkerchief tied over it. This had slipped at one corner and she thinks the index letters BU were visible. There was nobody in the car at the time."

MRS CATT   It just shows you, don't it? If Mr Fellowes 'adn't come into that little bit o' money - well, 'e might still be where you are. (*She hiccups.*) S'cuse me. Oh, it's no good - I shall 'ave to chuck it. (*She belches.*) Your pardon. (*She sits on the settee.*) I shall 'ave to 'ave a soda mint. (*She does.*) I 'aven't been the same woman since Sunday - when I 'ad that little bit of tinned lobster for me supper.

STEVE   D'you really think Mr Fellowes was murdered for his money?

MRS CATT   'E was a dark 'orse. You never knoo 'ow to take 'im. I daresay 'e got into bad company, and when a boy gets in bad company - I don't know what's the matter wiv me. (*Rising, restlessly.*) I can't seem to sit easy this mornin' some'ow.

STEVE   Why not?

MRS CATT   (*with dignity*) Never you mind.

               (DESCIUS *enters briskly from the house. He is
               no longer the haunted man. His is bright and
               alert - at his most dangerous.*)

DESCIUS   (*to* STEVE) What are you doing, Steve? Why
               aren't you in the shop?

STEVE   I was only reading about poor Mr Fellowes,
               sir.

DESCIUS   (*taking the newspaper*) Oh! So you're a crime
               fan, eh? (*He folds the newspaper into a
               convenient shape.*) There is only one use for a
               newspaper at your age, boy. To box one's ears
               - see? (*He proceeds to demonstrate the truth
               of this upon* STEVE.) Run along, run along.
               You're not to leave the counter till I tell you.

               (STEVE *goes into the shop.* DESCIUS *sits at his
               desk and begins to read* STEVE'S *newspaper,
               humming to himself.* MRS CATT *goes on with
               her work.*)

               (*looking up suddenly*) This is the first time
               you've swept this room out since Sunday,
               isn't it?

MRS CATT   (*on the defensive*) Well, and why not?
               Tuesdays, Thursdays and Saturdays is me
               cleanin' days for in 'ere. You can't keep
               forever o' cleanin'. Life's too short as it is.
               You can't always be kneeling about and my
               knees ain't none too good this morning.
               Listen. (*She raises one knee and works it up
               and down.*) Can you 'ear it crackin? You're
               too far away. (*She works it again.*) Come over
               'ere and you'll hear it. Why, I can play "God
               save the King" on 'em!

DESCIUS   Never mind your musical knees, Mrs Catt.
               Bring your dustpan over here.

MRS CATT   Eh? Wotever for?

DESCIUS   (*taking out a sheet of paper and laying it on
               the desk*) Empty it out on this clean sheet of
               paper. I dropped a diamond on the carpet on
               Sunday. (*She empties the dust on to the
               paper.*) A small brilliant.

MRS CATT   You needn't look at me like that. I 'aven't
               eaten it. Sad about poor Mr Fellowes, isn't it?

DESCIUS   (*examining the dust*) Yes. I'm afraid he must
               have made an enemy after he left my
               employment. (MRS CATT *attempts to finger the
               dust. He knocks her hand away.*) No, no. Keep
               your silly hands away! Dust can be dangerous.

MRS CATT   Yes, I know. Full o' microbes and 'obgoblins
               - if you believe in 'em. There it is!

               (*Again she tries to finger the dust. Again he
               knocks her hand away.*)

DESCIUS   There it isn't!

MRS CATT   I'm only trying to help yer. 'Ere! Wot about
               that little fing?

               (*She points to the dust.* DESCIUS *again tries to
               knock her hand away but she withdraws it. He
               only succeeds in striking his own hand against
               the desk. She chuckles.*)

MRS CATT   I was too quick for yer that time! Yes - Mr
               Fellowes was over-young ter die. 'E took
               quite a fancy to me. And, of course, that's
               fatal. I bring bad luck on young men. Always
               'ave.

DESCIUS   (*quite affably*) He called to see me on Sunday
               afternoon, they tell me. But I was too poorly

to talk to him. I wonder what he wanted to
say.

MRS CATT   It's too late to bother about that now. Any
luck?

DESCIUS   No, no. Nothing there.

            (*He tips the dust back into the pan.*)

MRS CATT   I'll keep me eyes skinned on Thursday.

DESCIUS   Let me go through the dust before you burn it.
            Do you understand? Every pan full.

            (MARGARET *enters from the house.*)

MARGARET   (*coming to her father*) Oh, you've got the
            morning paper! Is there anything more than in
            last night's?

DESCIUS   Yes. It's full of nothing else.

MRS CATT   Ain't it fair chronic?

DESCIUS   What is fair? What is chronic?

MRS CATT   The way the papers hadvertise these yer
            nashty murders.

DESCIUS   Oh - I think there can be something
            extraordinarily thrilling about them!

MRS CATT   (*making for the stairway*) Morbid, I calls it.
            'Arpin' on 'uman infirmity. (*She ascends the
            steps, in her dreariest manner.*) We oughter
            lift up our 'eads to the light instead of
            worrying about who done it, why they done it
            and are they going to do it again . . .

            (*She disappears.*)

MARGARET   (*reading the headlines*) "Youth's Body in a
            Ditch" . . . "Mystery Car by Roadside" . . .
            "Dunmow . . ." However did he get to
            Dunmow, Daddy?

DESCIUS	It looks, my darling, as though somebody took him for a ride.
MARGARET	You remember I told you about his calling here in the afternoon while you were upstairs?
DESCIUS	Yes.
MARGARET	I didn't tell you one thing. He had a revolver on him.
DESCIUS	Archie? A revolver? A boy like that? Oh no. You must have made a mistake.
MARGARET	No, I haven't. He, er, he took it out and showed us.
DESCIUS	You do surprise me. It almost looks as though he'd been afraid of somebody.

(ROBERT *enters*.)

ROBERT	Hullo, darling. Good morning, Poppa.
DESCIUS	Ah, here is my good physician! I am very much better, Robert. The spell is broken. I've had two good nights' sleep.
ROBERT	You look a different man altogether.
DESCIUS	I *am* a different man altogether.
MARGARET	And now, just when you're better, Aunt Mathilde must go and crack up! You *are* a couple!
DESCIUS	But Aunt Mathilde hasn't cracked up, has she?
MARGARET	She looks absolutely rotten.
DESCIUS	Well, this has upset her very much. She was very fond of Archie.

MARGARET   Yes, Daddy. But Aunt Mathilde was horribly
             seedy all yesterday, and we didn't know about
             Archie till the evening.

DESCIUS   True. True.

ROBERT   (*who has been scanning the newspaper*) I
             think we'd better go and get some more
             papers.

DESCIUS   Do. Do. Get some for me, too.

ROBERT   It's quite a new experience for me, Poppa.
             I've never been mixed up in a murder before.

DESCIUS   Well, I hope you're not now!

ROBERT   Oh, I've got a perfect alibi!

DESCIUS   (*slyly*) You make me feel as if I ought to rub
             up mine.

ROBERT   What paper do you want?

DESCIUS   Oh, get them all. Hang the expense! This
             doesn't happen every day, you know.

MARGARET   I should hope not. You *are* a funny old stick.
             This way, Robert.

             (*She kisses* DESCIUS *lightly, and she and*
             ROBERT *go out through the shop.* DESCIUS *takes
             up the paper.*)

DESCIUS   (*to himself*) A red car - make unknown - index
             letters BU . . .

             (AUNT MATHILDE *enters from the house. She is
             dressed for shopping and carries a basket.
             She looks white, strained and wretched.*)

             Oh, it's you!

MATHILDE   Yes. I'm off out to get some vegetables.

DESCIUS   (*watching her closely*) Better buy yourself a
               pot of rouge. If you're not careful, that white
               face of yours will give the game away.

MATHILDE   Descius, it's terrible - the strain. Terrible.

DESCIUS   Mathilde, we're in danger. Great danger. But
               we've a very good chance - if we don't betray
               ourselves.

MATHILDE   I can't think how you manage to stand up to it
               like you do.

DESCIUS   I'm always at my best when things are
               dangerous.

MATHILDE   Mother of God! And I am no help to you.

DESCIUS   (*tenderly*) My poor Mathilde . . .

MATHILDE   I've stood by you all your life. I've shared all
               the risks. I'll try not to let you down at the
               end.

DESCIUS   This isn't the end - besides, you won't let me
               down. (*He rises and kisses her.*) Little sister.
               After all, what have we done? We've only
               killed a snake.

               (STEVE *enters from the shop.*)

STEVE   A gentleman in the shop to see you, sir.

DESCIUS   Who is it?

STEVE   He wouldn't give his name.

DESCIUS   Right. Ask him in.

               (AUNT MATHILDE *peers through the glass in
               the door.*)

MATHILDE   Just a minute - it is all right.

               (STEVE *returns to the shop.*)

It's Morris! Descius, I can't meet him. I must go out the other way.

(*She scurries into the house.* CORDER MORRIS *enters from the shop. He is in a state of excitement and agitation.*)

MORRIS Have you seen it?

DESCIUS (*holding up the paper*) Do you mean this?

MORRIS (*feverishly, mopping his brow*) My God, they've got me!

DESCIUS (*still imperturbably reading the paper*) Don't be ridiculous.

MORRIS A red car - registration letters beginning BU!

DESCIUS (*sharply*) Sssh!

MORRIS (*sinking into a chair*) It won't be long before they get on to my little MG.

DESCIUS My dear Morris!

MORRIS Why the hell did I choose a red car? Oh, of course! My wife - the damn fool! She thought it looked fetching.

DESCIUS And where is it?

MORRIS Where I always keep it. In a private lock-up garage belonging to a friend's house.

DESCIUS Is he safe?

MORRIS He's doing . . . well, he won't be about for three years. His wife rents it me.

DESCIUS Does she know what make of car you run?

MORRIS I doubt if she's ever seen it. It's a corner house. The entrance to the garage is in a different road.

DESCIUS   Then aren't you perspiring a little too soon?

MORRIS   (*mopping his collar*) Wish I thought so.
                Number plate covered with a green silk
                handkerchief.

DESCIUS   (*noting his handkerchief*) Yes, I recommend
                you use pink in future.

                (MORRIS *stares at the handkerchief in horror,
                then stuffs it into his trouser pocket.*)

MORRIS   I never knew anyone passed us on the road,
                did you?   •

DESCIUS   I wasn't quite sure. It must have been while
                we were on the other side of the hedge. What
                are you going to do?

MORRIS   I'm going over to Belfast tomorrow. Then
                down to Eire for a bit.

DESCIUS
MORRIS   }   (*in unison*) Yeeeeessss.

MORRIS   An ugly thing, murder. Accessory after the
                fact, aren't I?

DESCIUS   Perhaps - if you wait a week or two - they'll
                be offering a pardon.

MORRIS   (*curtly*) I'm not that sort.

DESCIUS   I didn't think you were.

MORRIS   I wish to God I'd never been mixed up in it. If
                I hadn't left that blasted bag of mine behind,
                I'd have never called back for it. Never have
                been where I am now!

DESCIUS   (*slowly, blandly*) Morris, my dear boy, when
                you suggested killing Archie . . .

MORRIS   (*reflecting*) My God, you're right. So I did.

DESCIUS   It meant nothing to you. When I declined you
                called me yellow.

MORRIS   Yes, I did, I did.

DESCIUS   And yet when I was pushed over the edge and
                - with my own hands - did actually kill him -
                you, who merely helped me to dump the body
                - why, you're all to pieces. Your nerve is
                broken. Whereas I've never felt better, never
                stronger. Never more calm.

MORRIS   My God, it's true . . . How do you account for
                it?

DESCIUS   Because for me from now on it is a game. My
                one concern is . . . to win.

MORRIS   I wish you luck. I wish us both luck. Look
                here - I mustn't stop. I only wanted you to
                know my plans. I've a lot to do. Quite a lot to
                pack.

DESCIUS   (*detaining him as he tries to go*) You're not
                travelling with your wife, I hope? Couples are
                so easily traced.

MORRIS   I'm pushing her off to Cornwall for a bit. I've
                got a little hideout there.

DESCIUS   If you should want anything . . .

MORRIS   (*eagerly*) Thanks.

DESCIUS   (*suavely*) Communicate through Franck. And
                remember - there's nothing to be afraid of.

MORRIS   I hope you're right.

DESCIUS   (*significantly*) Except oneself.

                (ROBERT *and* MARGARET *return through the
                shop with their newspapers.*)

MARGARET   Oh - sorry, Daddy. We thought you were
                alone.

DESCIUS   It's all right, darling. My visitor is just going.
                (*To* MORRIS.) This is my daughter -

MORRIS   (*with a swift glance at* DESCIUS) Your
                daughter! I see!

DESCIUS   And her fiancé, Dr Graham . . . Mr Ratoff.

MORRIS   (*to* MARGARET) How do you do?

MARGARET   Very well, thanks.

ROBERT   (*to* MORRIS) Good morning.

MORRIS   How are you?

DESCIUS   Mr Ratoff is going to a fancy dress ball,
                aren't you?

MORRIS   No. Er, yes.

DESCIUS   Yes. He is going as Ivan the Terrible, and I
                am lending him this old shako to wear with
                his costume.

                (DESCIUS *lifts down a grotesque Russian
                headdress and claps it on* MORRIS' *head.*
                MORRIS *stands dumbfounded.*)

DESCIUS   Voilà!

ROBERT   Oh, yes. That's terrible all right.

                (MORRIS *removes the headdress, which he
                holds in his hand. With the exception of*
                MORRIS, *they are all now reading the
                newspapers.*)

DESCIUS   (*to* ROBERT *and* MARGARET) My Lord! You've
                bought up the bookstall! (*To* MORRIS *again.*)
                We're all very interested in this Dunmow
                case, Mr Ratoff.

MORRIS   Yes.

DESCIUS   The young man who was murdered used to be
                my assistant.

MORRIS   Yes.

DESCIUS   But I don't suppose you remember him?

MORRIS   Yes.

DESCIUS   No.

MORRIS   No.

MARGARET   Aren't these papers extraordinary? They all
                say the same thing in different words. Look!
                It says here he was strangled, and in this one
                throttled.

DESCIUS   Oh, but they're quite different methods.

ROBERT   There you are!

MARGARET   That's what Rob's been saying. But I'm sure
                he's wrong. He must be.

DESCIUS   No, no. He's quite right - technically
                speaking (*Taking out his clean handkerchief
                and demonstrating on* ROBERT.) If you strangle
                a person, you take a scarf or a stocking or a
                bit of string or something, and twist it round
                his neck - so, drawing it tight - see? But if
                you throttle him you use your naked hands -
                so.

                (DESCIUS *suddenly seizes* MORRIS *by the throat.*
                MORRIS, *who has been straining for a peep at
                the paper* ROBERT *is reading, shrieks in alarm.*
                DESCIUS *slaps him on the back and roars with
                laughter.* MORRIS *gradually recovers, and
                observes that* MARGARET *is watching him. He
                conveys to her that* DESCIUS *and he are always
                having fun like that.*)

MORRIS   Well, if you'll excuse me - er - I've got an
                    important business appointment. (*He puts on
                    the headdress by mistake.*) Good day, good
                    day. (*He hurries out through the shop just as
                    JOAN enters from the house.*)

JOAN   Well, I never! You have some very odd
                    customers!

DESCIUS   Don't I!

MARGARET   Have you seen these, Joan?

JOAN   (*taking one*) You've got 'em all, I see.
                    (*Reading a headline.*) "Boy's varnished finger
                    nails." Well, well, well! Archie couldn't have
                    made much more of a splash if he'd been
                    drowned, could he?

MARGARET   That's a rotten thing to say!

JOAN   Why? It's the sort of death he'd have chosen,
                    isn't it, Poppa?

DESCIUS   We can't say, can we?

MARGARET   How do you mean - "the sort of death he'd
                    have chosen"?

JOAN   Well, he liked to pose as a gangster - and now
                    he's been bumped off.

DESCIUS   I don't think you ought to sound quite so
                    cheerful about it.

ROBERT   There's no doubt he was in with some gang.
                    And they ousted him.

DESCIUS   (*with a shrug*) One theory is as good as
                    another - till we know.

JOAN   If we ever do.

DESCIUS   Oh, we shall know all right. The English
                    police may look foolish, but they're very,
                    very clever boys, really.

ROBERT   What made him come back here such an awful
              lot after he left?

DESCIUS   If you want my secret opinion, I fancy he had
              his eye on Margaret.

MARGARET   (*in amazement*) Daddy, don't be ridiculous!

DESCIUS   I thought that would make you sit up.

MARGARET   But he always came to see *you*.

DESCIUS   I'm afraid that was only a blind. He never
              talked about anything but you. And once he
              asked me if there was any chance of your
              engagement being broken off.

MARGARET   Oh, Daddy! Don't!

ROBERT   Did he, by God!

              (*To their astonishment,* MARGARET *suddenly
              breaks down.*)

DESCIUS   My darling! What have I said?

ROBERT   What's the matter?

MARGARET   (*controlling herself*) Oh, I don't know. It's
              my nerves, I suppose. The thought of it all's
              so horrible.

              (JOAN *starts collecting the newspapers in a
              very matter-of-fact fashion.*)

JOAN   I vote we give all the papers to Mrs Catt and
              forget about Master Archie,

              (STEVE *enters hurriedly.*)

STEVE   If you please, sir, there's a gentleman to see
              you. I keep telling him you're engaged, but he
              won't -

A VOICE   Good morning.

(*The voice belongs to a tall, well-built, rather fine-looking man of about thirty. He comes in from the shop, in* STEVE's *wake, bland and courteous, but not in any way to be controlled or barred or put off.* STEVE *retires.*)

Could I see Mr Descius Heiss?

DESCIUS   But yes! I am Mr Heiss.

ELLIOTT   (*producing a card*) My name's Elliott. Detective Inspector. Scotland Yard.

DESCIUS   Oh? Have you come to see me about my poor Archie?

ELLIOTT   Fellowes - the name. That's right. Archie Fellowes. The Dunmow case. I'm in charge of it.

DESCIUS   We have just been discussing it. (*Introducing the others.*) My daughter and her friend, Miss Deal. And her fiancé, Dr Graham.

ELLIOTT   (*eyeing* ROBERT) Robert Graham, is it? Good Lord!

ROBERT   (*very friendly*) Hullo John! (*They shake hands.*)

DESCIUS   Well, Robert, I never expected to see you recognised by Scotland Yard.

ROBERT   We took our first MB together.

ELLIOTT   You mean you took it.

ROBERT   What was it you went down on?

ELLIOTT   Oh, I forget. Some stupid trick on the medulla oblongata. It fed me up. So I drifted into the police.

DESCIUS   Well, well, well - this is quite a romance!

ELLIOTT   How many years is it since King's College?

ROBERT   Won't bear thinking of.

ELLIOTT   What are you doing these days?

ROBERT   Sailing the seven seas as a medicine man.

ELLIOTT   Good! Perhaps we can have the chance to
            reminisce later. Just now I've got to talk to
            Mr Heiss if he'll give me a few minutes.

ROBERT   Right. We'll go.

DESCIUS   No. Don't go, Robert. Mr Elliott, these young
            people may be useful because they saw my
            poor Archie a few hours before it happened.

ELLIOTT   Really? Then they may be able to throw some
            light on the question. No, please wait.

DESCIUS   Won't you sit down?

ELLIOTT   Thanks. So, Mr Heiss. You employed this
            boy, Fellowes, didn't you? For how long?

DESCIUS   About two years.

ELLIOTT   Where did his people live? We can't trace
            them.

DESCIUS   I believe he was an orphan. I never knew a
            great deal about him. He didn't talk very
            much.

ELLIOTT   I understand he left you because he came into
            money. Do you know how he got it?

DESCIUS   I've no idea. (*Appealing to the others.*) Did he
            say it was from an aunt or somebody? I've
            really no idea.

ELLIOTT   What were you paying him?

DESCIUS   Oh, quite a small weekly wage. Twenty five
           shillings or something. He was really learning
           the business.

ELLIOTT   What did you make of him?

DESCIUS   He assisted me in my shop.

ELLIOTT   I don't mean that. The boy himself - what was
           he like?

DESCIUS   He was a weak, rather girlish sort of boy. He
           worked well. I've no complaints.

ELLIOTT   Can you give me some idea of his tastes?

DESCIUS   He had something of an eye for beauty. He
           could tell a pretty piece of jewellery, for
           instance, if he saw one. I should have called
           him an artistic type.

ELLIOTT   A bit luxurious, I suppose.

DESCIUS   (*with a quiet, grim smile*) Not while he was
           with me.

ELLIOTT   (*referring to his notes*) All his underclothes -
           socks, shirts - were silk.

DESCIUS   Silk? Disgusting!

ELLIOTT   He went to one of the best tailors in Saville
           Row. His hat was a Heath. Gold cigarette
           case. His little flat, too. Very precious.

DESCIUS   I suppose he must have gone the pace a bit.
           Like a lot of young fellows with easy money.

ELLIOTT   Probably. Do you know anything about his
           movements after he left you?

           (AUNT MATHILDE *enters from the shop. Her
           basket is now full of vegetables. She hesitates
           when she sees the visitor.*)

           . . . Or what company he kept? Oh . . .

DESCIUS   My sister, Miss Mathilde - Mr Elliott.

ELLIOTT   (*politely*) How do you do?

DESCIUS   Mr Elliott is from Scotland Yard, Mathilde.
           He is enquiring about our poor Archie. Sit
           down, my dear.

MATHILDE   (*turning her white face imploringly to*
           DESCIUS) Must I?

DESCIUS   (*firmly*) Sit down. (*To* ELLIOTT.) My sister has
           felt it all very much. She was very fond of
           Archie. You will be able to refresh my
           memory, Mathilde. The smallest thing may
           sometimes be of the greatest importance,
           mayn't it, Mr Elliott?

ELLIOTT   It very often is. When did you last see him?

DESCIUS   About ten days ago. Or it may have been a
           fortnight. But he was in this house the night
           he was murdered.

ELLIOTT   Oh? But *you* didn't see him, you say?

DESCIUS   No, I was upstairs asleep. I've not been well.
           And Robert, who's my doctor, had sent me to
           lie down. But they saw him. The young
           people saw him.

ELLIOTT   What time was this?

MARGARET   About half past five. We'd just finished tea.
           We were getting ready to go to a sacred
           concert where I was playing the violin.

ELLIOTT   Did he call for any particular purpose?

MARGARET   I think it was to ask me to go to the opera
           with him.

DESCIUS   He was a little too fond of Margaret in my
           humble opinion.

MARGARET   That's nonsense!

ELLIOTT   Well, what happened?

MARGARET   He stayed for a little while. Then he went
                away. And we started off for the concert.

ROBERT   And, in case you've got anything on us, John,
                let me tell you here and now we've a perfect
                alibi. After the concert we went - all three of
                us - to supper at Lyon's Corner House.

ELLIOTT   (*dryly*) I *am* relieved. And that was the last
                time he was here?

DESCIUS   As far as I know, that was the last time.

ELLIOTT   Now, Mr Heiss, can you tell me *this* - Archie
                ran a banking account. There wasn't much in
                it - but there'd been a good deal through it.
                He opened it last August with a couple of
                thousand pounds. He paid them in notes.
                Notes for fifty and a hundred pounds each.
                Banks, you know, keep a record of the
                numbers of high-figured notes, and we've
                tracked them back. Most of them - though not
                all - had passed through your account and
                been drawn out by you earlier.

DESCIUS   (*in astonishment*) *My* account? Archie had
                money which had passed through my account!
                That's an extraordinary coincidence!

ELLIOTT   Oh, it's much more than a coincidence - it
                must be.

                (*The tension can almost be felt.* AUNT
                MATHILDE *is in agony. The young people are
                intensely interested.* DESCIUS *leaps to his feet
                in superbly feigned agitation.*)

DESCIUS   My God! My God!

MARGARET   Daddy! What's the matter?

DESCIUS   It's just occurred to me. Have I been robbed?
           (*For* ELLIOTT's *benefit*.) You see, in this
           business I have to keep quite a big sum on the
           premises. Where are my keys?

ELLIOTT   But, if he'd robbed you as long ago as last
           August, you'd have discovered it by now?

DESCIUS   Probably not. No - quite likely not. If he has
           been cunning, as I expect. Where are my . . .
           (*Produces his keys*.) Oh, here they are!

           (*He rushes feverishly to the safe, opens it and
           begins turning over its contents. These
           include several bundles of bank notes fastened
           by elastic bands to backings of cardboard,
           one or two account books, bags of coins,
           several little black velvet bags of loose
           stones, a couple of jewelled cups and
           ornaments and among the rest, oddly enough,
           the blowpipe and box of darts. The others
           watch him, spellbound.*)

           Now, let me see. No, no. That looks all right.
           This is here. This is here. One, two, three,
           four. Nothing seems missing. (*He lifts out a
           large gilt loving cup with a cover and carries
           it over to* MARGARET.) Look, Margaret. Help
           me. And you, Joan. This old loving cup is full
           of notes. Count them out. (*He returns to the
           safe*.) Reckon them up. Tell me what they
           amount to. It look all right to me, Mr Elliott.

MARGARET   (*who has taken off the lid*) But, Daddy,
           there's nothing in this. It's empty.

DESCIUS   (*rushing across*) Empty? Empty? Then I *have*
           been robbed!

JOAN   How much is missing?

DESCIUS   Thousands of pounds! Margaret - I'm ruined!

MARGARET   (*comfortingly*) Nonsense, darling!

DESCIUS	(*raging*) How dare she say nonsense! It's true, Mr Elliott, what you've been telling me. And my daughter says "nonsense"!
MARGARET	I didn't mean it like that, darling.
DESCIUS	I don't know what you meant! I only heard what you said!
MARGARET	All I meant, darling, is that it's only money.
DESCIUS	Only money? Where do you get these ideas from? It's my life's work he has taken!

(*He crosses to* MARGARET, *snatches the cup from her and stands holding it.*)

ROBERT	(*dryly, with a glance at what is left*) Oh, well, he hasn't got it all - apparently.
DESCIUS	That's not *his* fault. Be sure of that.
ELLIOTT	Do you keep all your money in the house?
DESCIUS	(*almost rudely*) Of course I don't. I run a banking account like everybody else. But the bulk of what I have is here.
ELLIOTT	Rather an extraordinary method, isn't it, for nowadays?
DESCIUS	Mr Elliott, I'm of French extraction. My father was a peasant. And, you know, in France, the peasant's bank is his stocking. Perhaps I inherit his ideas - I don't know. I don't mean I'm a miser. I don't count my money every day. I only balance my books once a year like everybody else.
ELLIOTT	Well, I'm afraid I've been proved right. I'm sorry it's been such a shock.
DESCIUS	A shock? A shock! (*Suddenly rounding on* AUNT MATHILDE.) And you can sit there stark and stupid like a stuffed monkey, and not say one little word?

MATHILDE   (*her teeth chattering*) It's terrible . . .

DESCIUS   Terrible? Is that all you can say? Somebody
            bring her a dictionary!

            (*He crosses to his desk, sets down the cup
            with a crash, and sinks into his chair.*)

ELLIOTT   (*concealing his amusement*) Half a minute.
            Let's be calm about it. We know now where
            he got the two thousand to open his account
            with. That's very helpful. (DESCIUS *appears to
            be in pain.*) But there's just one other point.

MARGARET   I wonder, Mr Elliott, couldn't you come back
            again? Daddy's been awfully seedy for some
            time. We've been afraid for his heart.

DESCIUS   (*testily*) Rubbish! I'm as fit as a fiddle. (*He
            rises and bows apologetically.*) Mr Elliott,
            I'm so sorry. I've made an exhibition of
            myself. You see, I *feel*! I'm not cold-blooded
            like you English. But I have courage. I can
            face facts - once they *are* facts. (*He sits
            again.*) Now, I'm quite ready to answer all
            your questions.

ELLIOTT   Well, then. This passage of notes from you to
            him didn't stop with the first two thousand.
            It's been going on all the time - ever since he
            left you. We've traced about four thousand
            pounds in all. Some as recently as a fortnight
            ago.

            (*The effect of this on* DESCIUS *is
            extraordinary. He rises, rushes to* AUNT
            MATHILDE *and seizes her by the shoulders,
            dragging her to her feet. His face is contorted
            with rage.*)

DESCIUS   You damned old fool! This is *your* doing! You
            always showed him in when he came! You
            always left him alone!

MARGARET   Daddy!

DESCIUS   (*to them*) Don't you see what's happened? He
                  must have taken an impression of my keys!
                  He's been robbing me all the time! Your
                  trustingness, your stupidity have ruined me!
                  Oh, I could tear your eyes out!

                  (*He begins to shake* AUNT MATHILDE *like a dog
                  shaking a rat.*)

MATHILDE   (*faintly*) Mother of God!

ROBERT   (*pulling him away and setting her free*)
                  Steady - steady!

MARGARET   Daddy! You've hurt her!

                  (*Released,* AUNT MATHILDE *falls to the ground.*
                  DESCIUS *is immediately contrite.*)

DESCIUS   (*bending over her*) Oh, Mathilde! What have I
                  done? I'm beside myself.

ROBERT   (*helping her to her feet*) Keep away from her -
                  for God's sake.

MATHILDE   It's all right. I'm not hurt. But he frightened
                  me. He is so violent.

DESCIUS   (*coming forward*) Mathilde . . .

MARGARET   (*sharply*) Daddy - do leave her alone. You'd
                  better come upstairs, darling.

                  (*With* JOAN'S *help she leads the dazed old
                  woman from the room.* DESCIUS *comes to*
                  ELLIOTT.)

DESCIUS   Mr Elliott, I'm so sorry. I apologise. (*Then
                  quite alertly.*) Have you the numbers of these
                  notes?

ELLIOTT   Oh, yes.

DESCIUS   Might I see them?

ELLIOTT   I haven't got them on me. They're in the
                police station, just round the corner.

DESCIUS   Oh, I see.

ELLIOTT   But in any case I was going to ask you to step
                round there with me, if you wouldn't mind.

DESCIUS   (*a little taken aback*) Were you? Oh, I see.

ELLIOTT   Then I could give you a list of the numbers.

DESCIUS   So you could! I don't know what I'm doing. I
                don't know what I've lost. I hardly know who
                I am.

ELLIOTT   Well, get your coat. And come along.

DESCIUS   My coat. Oh, yes. (*He meets* JOAN *returning.*)
                Oh, Joan! How is Aunt Mathilde?

JOAN   Margaret's taken her upstairs.

DESCIUS   How could I have blamed her? I'm so
                ashamed. So ashamed. Mathilde! Mathilde!

                (*He shuffles out, a seemingly broken man.*
                JOAN *comes down into the room.*)

ELLIOTT   (*to* ROBERT) Well, my son, you're taking on a
                queer old dove as a father-in-law.

ROBERT   Not queer. He's only foreign.

ELLIOTT   I've never seen any man make such a fuss.

ROBERT   Wait till someone tells you you've lost four
                thousand pounds.

ELLIOTT   (*laughing*) No one'll ever tell me that!
                Amazing! His hoarding all that money in his
                safe!

ROBERT   It's just on a par with everything. Look - he's
                left it all lying about now. He's simply a
                great baby. Of course, he's a fine connoisseur
                and judge of stones and all that. But in
                business matters he's a perfect child.

JOAN   (*dryly*) All the same, Robert, he's managed to
                put away quite a few ha'pennies in his little
                money box.

ROBERT   He's in a trade where, when you do make
                money, well, you make it.

ELLIOTT   That's true of all antique dealers. Besides, he
                goes in for pretty good stuff, you know. Look
                at that armour. Dutch, seventeenth century.
                (*He wanders over to it.*) I don't know when
                I've seen a finer morion. It's really lovely
                work.

ROBERT   I didn't know you knew anything about
                armour.

ELLIOTT   Oh, I do a little collecting - in my very small
                way. It's my hobby. Quieter than a wife and
                cheaper than a mistress. What's he asking for
                it? (*Examining the price label.*) Oh? Seventy
                five pounds! Cheap.

ROBERT   Sounds mighty dear to me.

ELLIOTT   (*casually*) He obviously thinks it's an Italian
                reproduction. He's probably right. (*Drawing
                something from his pocket.*) By the way,
                Robert. I fancy I've got something here in
                your line. You've been in the East, I expect?

ROBERT   Only backwards and forwards about three
                times a year.

ELLIOTT   (*showing him something*) We found this in the
                dead man's pocket. Can you tell me what it
                is?

ROBERT　　　　(*in a strange voice*) Yes. It's a Japanese netsuki button.

　　　　　　　(JOAN *stops lighting a cigarette and is instantly alert.*)

ELLIOTT　　　　Thought so. Carved ivory. Mice - or are they rats - on some sort of shell?

ROBERT　　　　Listen, John. I can tell you the whole story about that. I brought it home from Kobe only last week, and gave it to old Heiss to sell for me. When Archie Fellowes called here last Sunday I caught him trying to pinch it.

ELLIOTT　　　　That bears out our friend's idea of his being a thief.

ROBERT　　　　Exactly. What do you that of that, Joan? He must have picked it up again before he left - the little shyster - when my eye didn't happen to be on him.

ELLIOTT　　　　I see. Thought I'd got on to something. Evidently I haven't.

ROBERT　　　　It's my property. I suppose I can have it back one day?

ELLIOTT　　　　Of course. After the inquiry. Or the trial, if there is one.

　　　　　　　(DESCIUS *enters. He is wearing a black Homburg hat and a neat black overcoat. He looks like a respectable City merchant.*)

DESCIUS　　　　I'm quite ready, Mr Elliott. (*Surveying the litter on the floor.*) Oh, dear! What a careless old fool I am. Here are all my things all over the place. Take my keys, Robert. (*He hands them to him.*) Put them back for me, there's a dear boy. (*With watery humour.*) And mind you don't steal too much.

ROBERT	Oh, I shall only skim the cream.
DESCIUS	Joan, you help him - and keep your eye on him. Come, Mr Elliott. I mustn't be away long. Tuesday is a very busy day in the shop. Oh, dear. I wish it were still Monday.
ELLIOTT	Why?
DESCIUS	Because, if it were, I shouldn't have found out I'd been robbed till tomorrow.

(*He and* ELLIOTT *go out through the shop. There is a pause.* ROBERT *begins to put things back into the safe. He notices* JOAN *does not attempt to help. She looks very strange.*)

ROBERT	(*to* JOAN) Here! This was to be a fifty-fifty job, you know.
JOAN	(*in a queer voice*) Robert -
ROBERT	Hullo?
JOAN	There's something . . . very serious . . .
ROBERT	(*struck by her tone*) What?
JOAN	Archie came back here on Sunday - after he left. They're lying.
ROBERT	Who are lying?
JOAN	Mr Heiss and Aunt Mathilde. That little netsuki. It was still here on Sunday when we left for the concert.
ROBERT	(*astonished*) Are you sure?
JOAN	(*crossing to the mantelpiece*) Absolutely certain. I picked it up myself from the tea table after Archie had gone, and laid it in this tray - here - on the mantelpiece. (*She touches the tray, and as she does so, starts - but she goes on.*) Now it's been found in Archie's

pocket. So he *must* have come back. He *must* have.

ROBERT   That's odd. But why should they lie about it?

JOAN   That's what I'd like to know. And all this rumpus just now about the money. The old man was just putting up an act. He *knew* the money wasn't there before he opened the safe.

ROBERT   (*turning and resuming his work of putting things back into the safe*) Aren't you being a little to . . . imaginative?

(JOAN *returns to the mantelpiece and, as she speaks, unseen by him, she tries to lift several of the ornaments, without success.*)

JOAN   If he'd really believed he'd been robbed, he'd have rushed straight to the safe and opened it. And he'd have done it without a word. And then why did he turn on Aunt Mathilde like that?

ROBERT   Well - as he said, he was beside himself.

JOAN   (*coming to him again*) Oh, no, he wasn't. I watched her from the moment she came in. She was on the verge of a collapse the whole time. He wanted to get her out of the room.

ROBERT   You have got a down on poor old Poppa!

JOAN   (*helping him*) I haven't. I'm awfully fond of them all. Margaret's my best friend. I wouldn't have anything happen to them for the world. But whatever's at the back of it, they're playing a very odd game. Don't *you* think so?

ROBERT   (*with a smile*) I think you're being very energetic mentally. But, even supposing you're right, what's at the back of it?

JOAN   I shouldn't be running round in circles if I
                knew. Anyhow, I thought it was a darned
                good job Elliott turned out to be a friend of
                yours.

ROBERT   (*his tone changing suddenly*) Why, d'you
                suppose, he asked Poppa to go to the station
                with him?

JOAN   Did he? (*Her tone changes too.*) Robert, you
                don't think he suspects Mr Descius?

ROBERT   No, of course not. (*Suddenly, directly.*) Look
                here. Do you?

JOAN   No, of course not. But he's hiding something.
                Something to do with Archie.

ROBERT   What?

JOAN   I think he's been paying that young man
                money - lots of money - and he doesn't want
                anyone to know it.

ROBERT   An old man like that - paying Archie?

JOAN   I'm fond of Mr Descius . . . you can't help
                being - but I wouldn't trust him an inch. Now,
                I'm going to ask you one other thing.

ROBERT   Well?

JOAN   Lift me down that little tray from the
                mantelshelf, will you?

ROBERT   This?

JOAN   Never mind the tray. Lift me down something
                else. The clock, or those statuettes.

ROBERT   (*trying unsuccessfully*) That's funny - why,
                the whole darned lot's screwed down.

JOAN   I thought so. I tried to lift up the tray just
                now, when I was telling you about the
                netsuki. It wouldn't budge.

ROBERT   (*examining them*) You're quite right. It's
              screwed down. Everything on the mantelpiece
              is screwed down. If you look underneath,
              there are the screws puttied over and painted.

JOAN   Well, that's a bit odd, isn't it?

ROBERT   He probably doesn't like his things moved.
              We'll have to ask Margaret. (*Returning to his
              work.*) How long have you known them?

JOAN   Ever since I was a kid.

ROBERT   You've never had any feelings about them
              until now?

JOAN   I don't know that I should have *now*. Except
              that Mr Descius took such a lot of pains to
              make himself look such a fool.

ROBERT   (*taking up the blow pipe and box*) I don't
              know what this blowpipe's doing here. It
              doesn't belong here. It belongs over there.

              (*He puts them back on top of the radio. JOAN
              is now sitting on the settee and lighting a
              cigarette. MARGARET enters. She goes to a
              drawer in the desk.*)

ROBERT   Well, how's the old lady?

MARGARET   I'm going to give her a little sal volatile. That
              can't hurt her, can it?

ROBERT   Good Lord, no.

MARGARET   (*finding it in the drawer*) I'm frightfully
              angry with Daddy.

JOAN   I don't think he really meant it.

ROBERT   He's sorry enough about it now.

MARGARET   (*going to the door*) What's the good of being
              sorry afterwards? People ought to be sorry
              before.

ROBERT   I say, there's something I want to ask you.

MARGARET   I'll be back in a minute.

              (*She goes out with the sal volatile.*)

ROBERT   What's the matter?

              (JOAN *is displaying the symptoms of distress
              usual in women who are afraid for their
              clothes.*)

JOAN   I'm caught on something. A nail or
              something. Behind my shoulder. (*She
              wriggles free.*) It's all right. I'm free. I don't
              think there's any damage.

ROBERT   (*he crosses to the settee*) Where is it?

JOAN   I don't know. It's somewhere here. There it is
              - look. Sticking in the settee. There.

              (ROBERT *bends and looks at it closely.*)

ROBERT   (*in an odd voice*) Wait a minute. Don't touch
              it.

              (*All his lightness has now gone. From this
              moment he takes the initiative. His face
              changes. He crosses to the desk, takes up the
              jewellers' forceps, returns to the settee and
              carefully extracts the dart.*)

              (*almost to himself*) Good God, it's gone in
              deep. There was some force behind that. (*To
              JOAN.*) It was the blunt end that caught your
              dress. Look. Do you see what it is?

JOAN   Why, it's a thorn.

ROBERT   (*carrying it in the forceps very carefully over
              to the box*) It's one of those blowpipe darts.
              (*He drops the dart in.*) The other's in here.

JOAN	(*she is strained, too, as well*) What! Your curare things?
ROBERT	(*after a moment*) It's been fired at somebody.
JOAN	(*instantly, wide-eyed*) Archie?
ROBERT	Archie.
JOAN	It - it couldn't have been done for fun, could it?
ROBERT	(*grimly*) No. Believe me, it's never done for fun.
	(ROBERT *goes to the bell and rings it.*)
JOAN	What are you doing?
ROBERT	I'm going to ask a question.
JOAN	Only one person can have fired it.
ROBERT	I'll tell you if you're right - in a minute.
JOAN	But Archie wasn't poisoned. He was throttled.
	(MRS CATT *enters.* ROBERT *picks up* AUNT MATHILDE'S *basket of vegetables.*)
ROBERT	Ah, Mrs Catt. Miss Mathilde asked me to give you these.
MRS CATT	(*taking the basket*) The vegetables! Oh, they're there, are they? I've gotter get on with the lunch. I've been looking for 'em everywhere.
ROBERT	(*casually*) Do you know if Descius found what he's been looking for?
MRS CATT	D'yer mean 'is little diamond?
ROBERT	Oh, so it was a little diamond, was it?
MRS CATT	Yes. No, 'e ain't found it - not yet. I'm to bring 'im the dust every time I sweeps the

room out so's 'e can go through it with 'is
magnifying glasses.

ROBERT   I see. (*Changing the subject.*) I wish you'd
              tell me something that's always been a puzzle
              to me. Why are all those chimney ornaments
              screwed down?

MRS CATT   Ask me another. That's another of 'is
              lordship's little tantrums. 'E's very partikler
              nothink shouldn't ever be moved off o' that
              chimney piece.

ROBERT   I've never noticed it before. It isn't the same
              all over the house, surely?

MRS CATT   Oh, no. It's on'y just in 'ere. But this is 'is
              private sanctum. 'Is 'Oly of 'Olies, I calls it.
              'E can do wot 'e likes in 'ere, and the rest of
              us 'as gotter put up with it.

ROBERT   I think it's rather a neat idea. We do it aboard
              ship.

MRS CATT   Ho! It isn't honly the hornaments. You can't
              take that there little pitchur off the wall to
              dust it - not for love nor money. (*Indicating
              the miniature.*) 'E won't 'ave it moved. It's
              nailed to the wall. (*As she goes to the door.*)
              But I get even with the old 'Ottentot. I never
              so much as bother to touch it with my duster!
              'E can damn well dust it 'imself.

              (*She departs, chuckling, with the vegetables.
              There is a moment's pause.* JOAN *and* ROBERT
              look at each other. Then JOAN *tries to lift
              down the miniature.*)

JOAN   It is. It's fastened to the wall.

ROBERT   None of the other pictures are, are they? (*He
              tests one.*) No. (*He thinks for a moment.*) Hold
              on! I've got an idea! I wonder . . .

(*He begins to manipulate the miniature.* JOAN *watches him with the most intense interest. Suddenly under his handling the miniature swings round till it is upside down. The fireplace flies open like a door. The recess is revealed. There is a tense pause.* ROBERT *gives a prolonged whistle.* JOAN *peers in.* ROBERT *goes into the recess.*)

JOAN   Robert! What is he? A coiner?

ROBERT   Wait a minute. Let's think. An electric furnace. Crucibles. Moulds. No, there's no press. He's not a coiner.

(*He comes out of the recess.*)

JOAN   He melts things. Robert, I've got it. He's a receiver! A re-setter. That's what he is.

ROBERT   And Archie found it out! (*He shuts the fireplace by re-locking the miniature.*) Blackmail, then.

JOAN   (*her voice trembling*) And that means . . .

ROBERT   Oh, we've got a long way beyond boggling at it.

JOAN   Murder. My God! (*A pause.*) What have I done? Robert, what have I done?

ROBERT   (*grimly*) You've started a hare and damn well caught it.

JOAN   It's this beastly prying mind of mine . . . Whatever happens, we must keep this from Margaret.

ROBERT   Good God, yes.

JOAN   (*now very agitated*) Look here. I can't stop. I shall give it away.

ROBERT   (*quietly*) It's up to me to save her from knowing - If I can.

JOAN

I've done all the harm anyone could possibly do to their best friend.

(MARGARET *returns with the sal volatile bottle.*)

MARGARET

Joan darling, what's the matter? You look absolutely rotten.

JOAN

Do I? I suppose this beastly business is beginning to get me down too.

MARGARET

Now, don't start losing your head like Aunt Mathilde.

JOAN

I'll try not to. Though it might be better if I had. Look here, darling, I must go or I shall be late for my job. I . . . I'll try and call back this evening.

MARGARET

Perhaps we shall have something to tell you then.

JOAN

Perhaps you will. (*She gives a meaning look towards* ROBERT *and goes.*)

MARGARET

(*putting the bottle back in the drawer*) What was it you wanted to ask me?

ROBERT

(*with assumed vagueness*) I wanted to ask *you*, darling?

MARGARET

You said you wanted to ask me something when I was going out of the door.

ROBERT

Did I? Oh, Lord, I've clean forgotten!

MARGARET

(*charmingly*) You are an old nit-wit. (*Brightly.*) Where's Daddy gone?

ROBERT

Round to the police station with Elliott.

MARGARET

Why?

ROBERT   They're going to give him particulars of the
          stolen notes.

MARGARET I see. Robert, I don't think I'm an heiress any
          longer. Do you mind? (*She kneels on the
          settee.*)

ROBERT   Yes, I mind awfully. So much that I think we
          ought to get married right away.

MARGARET Do you, darling? All right. Well, try to look
          more cheerful about it. After all, it *was* your
          suggestion.

ROBERT   Wasn't I looking cheerful?

MARGARET No. You were looking jolly gloomy.

ROBERT   That's because I've got a good poker face.
          This is how I really feel about it. (*He kisses
          her.*)

MARGARET Darling. I *do* love you so much!

ROBERT   And I've never loved you more than I do
          today.

MARGARET Why today of all days?

ROBERT   Well, because somehow I feel you need
          strength, protection.

MARGARET There's nothing particularly weak about *me*.
          Anyway, Daddy protects me - not that I am
          refusing your offer. Darling, you *are* sweet,
          but you look so absurdly worried.

ROBERT   You do know, don't you, that you can count
          on me whatever happens - always?

MARGARET I don't think I've quite got this. What's
          behind that remark?

ROBERT   Just that - well, you know we aren't quite out
          of the woods yet over this murder.

MARGARET	I didn't know we were in a wood. It's nothing to do with us.
ROBERT	No, but it might become something to do with us. There's a sort of stigma attached to everyone who's connected with a murder.
MARGARET	I don't admit that we *are* connected with it. But the police will solve it, you'll see. I'm sure they will. Won't they, Daddy?

(*For* DESCIUS *has entered the shop. His manner is cheerful and brisk.*)

DESCIUS	Won't they what?
MARGARET	The police. They'll find out who killed Archie?
DESCIUS	Nothing could surprise me after today.
MARGARET	Robert says they won't.

(ROBERT *lights his pipe and sits on the settee.*)

DESCIUS	I've just come from the police station. What a wonderful force they are! Do you know, the place was so clean I could have eaten my breakfast off the floor.
MARGARET	Wasn't that nice? But I'm afraid it won't bring your money back.
DESCIUS	No. (*Taking off his coat and hat and giving it to her.*) Hang these up for me, my darling. No, it won't bring my money back. But didn't I tell you? I've decided to be a philosopher about it.

(MARGARET *takes his coat and hat.*)

MARGARET	I ought to scold you for being so unkind to Aunt Mathilde.

DESCIUS   No. Don't do that. Don't scold me. (*He moves
               up to her.*) I've had a very trying day. Make a
               fuss of your old papa. (*She kisses him.*) Now,
               one more for luck. (*She kisses him again and
               mounts the stairs, standing on the second
               step. He sees his keys and pockets them.*) Ah,
               the good Robert has done my job for me.
               Thank you, Robert.

MARGARET   There's a chicken for lunch. How'd you like it
               cooked?

DESCIUS   A chicken! Oh! (*Rubbing his hands.*) Let's
               have it Bonne Femme. And don't forget the
               little bit of garlic. Chicken Bonne Femme -
               that is what I should choose for my last meal
               if I were going to be guillotined.

MARGARET   (*gaily, going to the door*) You won't ever be
               that!

DESCIUS   You are encouraging!

MARGARET   (*mischievously*) No. They hang people in this
               country.

               (*She goes.* DESCIUS' *face grows grim for a
               moment, then lightens. He chuckles.*)

DESCIUS   (*to* ROBERT) Did you hear that? You happy
               dog! You're marrying a woman with that most
               priceless gift - a sense of humour. (*There is a
               slight pause.*)

ROBERT   They didn't keep you quite as long as you
               thought at the station. Did they?

               (DESCIUS *has sat down. He takes a small
               notebook from his pocket and is doing some
               arithmetic with the aid of a pencil.*)

DESCIUS   No. I made a little statement and signed it
               with a little pen. And I got the numbers of the

notes. I should think I'm five thousand
pounds down.

ROBERT   I always said you were a lucky man.

DESCIUS   (*with a wry face*) What is there so lucky in
            that?

ROBERT   I wish I could afford to say "I'm five
            thousand pounds down."

DESCIUS   Well, you *can* say it. You are! After all - what
            do I work for? Margaret! Who is going to be
            Margaret's husband? *You* are! My poor
            fellow. I'm extremely sorry for you. You *are*
            five thousand pounds down.

ROBERT   (*drily*) Thanks. (*With a change of tone.*) Did
            you never suspect Archie and these constant
            visits of his?

DESCIUS   No. Why should I?

ROBERT   Margaret and I did. You'll laugh when I tell
            you. We thought you were in Queer Street,
            and Archie was financing you.

DESCIUS   (*with a flash of pride*) But my dear Robert,
            I'm a rich man. Well, when I say rich, I mean
            comparatively speaking. (*Very casually.*) I
            dare say I'm worth fifty thousand pounds.

ROBERT   Perhaps it's just as well we didn't know that.
            Because I expect, if we had, we should have
            thought he was blackmailing you.

            (DESCIUS *drops his notebook and stoops to
            retrieve it.*)

DESCIUS   Blackmailing *me*? But you can only blackmail
            people who've got something to hide!

ROBERT   Haven't you? Nearly everybody's got
            something to hide. We thought it was Archie
            who was the cause of your not sleeping.

DESCIUS   Good gracious me! Did you think I was a
               wicked old man?

ROBERT   (*dropping his banter*) I *know* you're a wicked
               old man.

               (DESCIUS *stares at him in surprise.*)

ROBERT   D'you remember that little ivory netsuki I
               gave you to sell for me? Mice on a clam
               shell?

DESCIUS   Yes.

ROBERT   The police found it in Archie's pocket.

DESCIUS   What of it? He must have stolen it. He was in
               here on Sunday afternoon. You saw him.

ROBERT   It couldn't have been then. Because Joan
               remembers leaving it on the mantelpiece
               when we three went out to that concert. It was
               the last thing she did.

DESCIUS   Well, either she's made a mistake or -

ROBERT   Or Archie came back later that evening.

               (*There is a tense pause.*)

DESCIUS   (*slowly*) And which would you say is the more
               likely alternative?

               (*For an answer*, ROBERT *takes up the box
               containing the poison darts and lays it down
               in front of* DESCIUS.)

ROBERT   Open that.

               (DESCIUS *takes up the box, rattles it, then
               opens it. He sees the two darts. His face is a
               study.*)

DESCIUS   (*significantly*) Oh. (*There is a silence.*) I lost one of these. Where did you find it?

ROBERT   It was sticking in the back of the settee.

DESCIUS   (*with a wicked smile*) Now, how on earth did it get there, d'you imagine?

ROBERT   Do you really want me to tell you?

DESCIUS   No, dear boy. Sometimes, in my business, it doesn't pay to be too inquisitive.

ROBERT   It didn't pay with Archie either, did it?

DESCIUS   Not altogether. Robert, many years ago, when I was a young man, I fell in love with a very beautiful girl. I was friendly with her father. They were a devoted family. Unfortunately, he was a little bit shady. But they didn't know. He was rather fond of forging cheques. He was rather good at it. At last he was caught. He didn't disclose his real name. And the police never found it out. He got ten years. He died in prison. His family thought he had deserted them. But, of course, I knew. I visited him before his trial. He knew he would be found guilty. He knew he could not outlive his sentence. He asked me if I were prepared to go on with my marriage to his daughter, and, if so, whether I would promise to keep her in ignorance of his trouble. I said "yes." I swore it to him. And I kept my word. Now, if you had been in my shoes, what would you have done? Supposing she had been Margaret, for instance?

ROBERT   (*quietly, sincerely*) I should do the same.

DESCIUS   Thank you.

ROBERT   The point is, I'm not quite sure *how* to keep it from Margaret.

DESCIUS   Perhaps I can help you there.

ROBERT   I shall be grateful if you can.

DESCIUS   Suppose you tell me just how much you do
                 know.

ROBERT   Very well - if you insist. You killed Archie,
                 didn't you? (*There is no answer.*) Because
                 he'd been blackmailing you, hadn't he? (*No
                 answer.*) Because for many years you've been
                 a receiver of stolen goods - a re-setter - a
                 melter - haven't you? And Archie found out?
                 (*Still no answer.*) I don't know *how* - probably
                 just as I've found it out.

                 (*He turns and manipulates the miniature and
                 the fireplace swings forward, not enough to
                 disclose the furnace, but enough to show that
                 he knows the whole of* DESCIUS' *secret.*)

                 You tried to kill him first with a dart. But you
                 failed. So you had to kill him your own way.
                 The point it - you *had* to kill him. You *did*
                 kill him. Won't you answer?

                 (*There is a pause. Then* DESCIUS *rises and
                 speaks with real dignity.*)

DESCIUS   Do you know why I killed him? It was his last
                 demand. He wanted Margaret.

ROBERT   Margaret?

DESCIUS   He wanted me to force her to marry him.
                 (*With a half-smile.*) You see, it might have
                 been worse. (*He has walked to the fireplace.*)
                 Have you finished with this? I usually keep it
                 closed. (*He turns the miniature and bolts the
                 mantelpiece back into its position. He watches*
                 ROBERT *cunningly.*) It was lucky your knowing
                 Elliott. It made everything much easier.

ROBERT   You don't think it's possible he'll - come
              back?

DESCIUS   Not unless he discovers something fresh.
              And that might make it simpler, in the long
              run . . . for both of us.

              (*The house door opens silently and* AUNT
              MATHILDE *enters.*)

              They say murderers often dream about their
              victims. Archie won't make my nights very
              pleasant.

              (*The door shuts.* AUNT MATHILDE *comes
              forward. Both men turn to her.*)

MATHILDE   Descius!

DESCIUS   (*to her*) He knows.

MATHILDE   (*turning wildly to* ROBERT) Robert?

DESCIUS   It's all right. He's on our side.

ROBERT   But I'll have to make one condition. I think
              you'll have to retire and keep chickens in the
              country.

DESCIUS   I have been thinking that myself. My only
              trouble is that I am not fond of chickens. -
              except of course, on the table.

MATHILDE   Does that mean we're safe?

DESCIUS   Unless Mr Elliott is cleverer than I give him
              credit for. (*With quiet delight.*) Oh, Mathilde,
              I fooled the police to the top of their hats! I
              wish you'd been at the station. It would have
              appealed to your artistic sense. Why, Mr
              Elliott, you *are* back soon!

(*For the shop door had opened and* INSPECTOR ELLIOTT *enters quietly. Instantly the atmosphere becomes electric.*)

ELLIOTT   I'm afraid so, Mr Heiss. Rather a habit with bad pennies, you know.

DESCIUS   Do sit down. Have a cigar?

(ELLIOTT *is waved into a chair, but he declines the cigar.* AUNT MATHILDE *watches the scene as though fascinated.*)

ELLIOTT   No, thanks. I'll have a cigarette, if I may.

(*He takes one of his own.* DESCIUS *is standing at his desk. He selects a cigar for himself. He picks up the poison dart box and plays with it as if it were a match box.* ELLIOTT *is seated between him and* ROBERT. AUNT MATHILDE *is standing, almost cringingly, by the window.*)

DESCIUS   You don't smoke cigars?

ELLIOTT   Oh, sometimes. But not just now, if you don't mind.

DESCIUS   Then let me give you a word of advice - I'm always telling my American friends -

(*He now had the dart box open and one of the darts in his hand.*)

But I mustn't take up your time, Inspector. You're a very busy man.

ELLIOTT   (*with a half smile*) That's all right. I'm in no hurry now.

DESCIUS   (*watching him intently*) No, I suppose not. What a funny life yours must be, Inspector!

ELLIOTT   In what way?

DESCIUS   In all sorts of ways. Tell me. When you arrest
                people they usually go quietly, don't they?

ELLIOTT   That depends. More often than not. Of course,
                we take precautions.

                (*At this moment the figure of a helmeted
                policeman appears outside the window. He
                takes up his stand with his back to the room.
                AUNT MATHILDE gives a little gasp and drops
                her handbag.*)

MATHILDE   Ah . . .

                (DESCIUS' *gaze follows hers. He reacts
                covertly. She crosses to the settee and sits on
                it, almost cowering. Her back is to the others.
                ELLIOTT turns towards her in surprise.*)

DESCIUS   (*to* ELLIOTT - *significantly*) Of course. You
                must.

                (*He puts down his cigar deliberately, and
                plunges the point of the dart deep into his left
                palm, unseen by* ELLIOTT *and* AUNT MATHILDE.
                *He winces with the first pain. He closes the
                fingers of his left hand over the dart, and sits
                down again.* ROBERT *has seen him. He stiffens,
                but, meeting the old man's eyes, keeps silent.*)

DESCIUS   But sometimes, I suppose, they manage to
                cheat the hangman?

ELLIOTT   Not very often.

DESCIUS   Well, let's come to business, Inspector. What
                can I do for you?

ELLIOTT   (*sauntering to the shop door*) It's about this
                suit of Dutch armour. What's the lowest you'd
                take for it?

                (*The shock of this casual announcement
                staggers both* DESCIUS *and* ROBERT. *But the old*

curio dealer quickly masters himself. AUNT
MATHILDE *turns around with relief and
interest. The policeman outside saunters away
along the lonely street.*)

DESCIUS   To you - twenty pounds.

ELLIOTT   (*surprised*) But it's marked much more than
that.

DESCIUS   I know. But I've lost my capital, so I'm
starting a clearance sale.

ELLIOTT   (*examining the armour*) Good! I'll have it.

DESCIUS   (*bursting into roars of laughter which has
something ghastly about it*) Ha! Ha! Ha!
Please forgive me. I don't mean to be rude. It
just struck me as extremely funny. A
policeman collecting armour!

           (*The laughter has become almost a howl. It is
terrible.* AUNT MATHILDE *eyes him with
alarm.*)

MATHILDE   Descius!

           (*In the midst of his laughter the old man
suddenly stops. He rises. His face is contorted
with momentary anguish.*)

DESCIUS   Margaret!

           (*He slumps heavily across his desk.* AUNT
MATHILDE *screams.* ROBERT *and* ELLIOTT *hurry
to him. The former makes a brief
examination.*)

ROBERT   Dead. (*To* ELLIOTT.) Heart.

MATHILDE   Mother of God!

ROBERT   (*to* ELLIOTT - *away*) Just see no one comes in
from the shop for a minute, will you?

ELLIOTT   Of course. (*As he departs.*) Poor old fellow . . .

                 (*He goes out quickly into the shop.* ROBERT
                 unclenches DESCIUS' *left hand. There, in the
                 flesh, is sticking the little black dart. He takes
                 up the tweezers and deftly extracts it.*)

ROBERT   (*in a tense whisper*) You see? He killed
                 himself.

MATHILDE   Just when he was safe!

                 (*He drops the dart back in the box and lays it
                 once more on the desk. The house door is
                 flung open and* MARGARET *rushes in.*)

ROBERT   (*meeting her*) My darling - you've got to be
                 very brave.

MARGARET   (*thrusting by him and going to* DESCIUS)
                 Daddy! (*As she realises he is dead.*) Daddy!
                 (*Then, with almost a scream.*) No! No! No!

                 (AUNT MATHILDE *comes to* MARGARET *and takes
                 her in her arms.* MARGARET *bursts into wild
                 sobbing.*)

MATHILDE   Don't cry, my little one, don't cry. You see,
                 he might have been - (*She checks herself, then
                 begins again.*) He might have been - a
                 complete invalid.

                 Blackout.

PROPERTY PLOT

ACT ONE

On Stage: Jeweller's eyeglass - DESCIUS
Ring - DESCIUS
Keys - DESCIUS
Tickets - DESCIUS
Revolver - DESCIUS
Cigarette - JOAN
Tray of trinkets on desk - DESCIUS
Papers on floor - MRS CATT
White handkerchief - DESCIUS
Black velvet bag full of gems in safe - DESCIUS
Sheet of white paper - DESCIUS
Jeweller's forceps - DESCIUS
Bank notes - DESCIUS
Box of cigars - DESCIUS
Match - DESCIUS
Iron Tray - DESCIUS
Iron tongs, moulds and black eye shade - DESCIUS
Black crucible - DESCIUS

Off Stage: Brooch - ARCHIE
Gloves - MATHILDE
Suitcase - ROBERT
Containing: Miniature teapot in black bronze
Netsuki
Gilt image of Buddha
Oriental box
Darts and blow pipe
Necklace
Oriental newspaper
Sales book and till drawer - ARCHIE
Cashbook and till - ARCHIE
Bright coloured handkerchief - MORRIS
Pocketbook - MORRIS

ACT TWO

On Stage: Tea and crumpets on table
Violin case - MARGARET
Pipe and tobacco - ROBERT
Netsuki - ARCHIE
Blow pipe and box of darts on piano - DESCIUS
Penknife - ROBERT
Cigar - DESCIUS
Newspaper - MATHILDE
Crucible - MATHILDE
Keys in pocket - DESCIUS
Bank notes from safe - DESCIUS

Off Stage: Violin - MARGARET
Cigarette case - ARCHIE
Revolver - ARCHIE
Black Gladstone bag - MORRIS
Containing: Gold boxes
          Gold bottle tops
          Smashed and twisted gold
Bottle - MRS CATT

ACT THREE

On Stage: Newspaper - STEVE
Feather duster - STEVE
Dustpan and brush - MRS CATT
Sheet of paper - DESCIUS
Grotesque Russian head-dress - DESCIUS
In safe: Bundles of bank notes, bags of coins,
        jewelled cups, loving cup filled with
        notes, bag of stones, blowpipe and box of
        darts in safe - DESCIUS
Cigarette - JOAN
Medicament - MARGARET
Dart - ROBERT
Jeweller's forceps - ROBERT
Bunch of keys - DESCIUS
Cigar - DESCIUS

Off Stage: Basket - MATHILDE
                Green silk handkerchief - MORRIS
                Newspapers - MARGARET and ROBERT
                White handkerchief - DESCIUS
                Card - ELLIOTT
                Shopping basket filled with vegetables - MATHILDE
                Japanese netsuki in pocket - ELLIOT
                Sal volatile bottle - MARGARET
                Pipe and matches - ROBERT
                Small notebook and pencil - DESCIUS
                Handbag - MATHILDE